A Talent Lost/ A Life with a Purpose

The Linda Dale Story

by
Linda (Dale) Cook

PublishAmerica
Baltimore

© 2007 by Linda (Dale) Cook.
All rights reserved. No part of this book may be reproduced, stored in a retrieval system or transmitted in any form or by any means without the prior written permission of the publishers, except by a reviewer who may quote brief passages in a review to be printed in a newspaper, magazine or journal.

First printing

ISBN: 1-4241-7198-9 (softcover)
ISBN: 978-1-4489-7778-9 (hardcover)
PUBLISHED BY PUBLISHAMERICA, LLLP
www.publishamerica.com
Baltimore

Printed in the United States of America

This book is dedicated to the memory of my beautiful grandson,
Jacob Lyle Woods.
November 1, 1985 — March 4, 2007

                          Linda A. Cook

Acknowledgments

I would first like to acknowledge my hero, the man responsible for utilizing cutting-edge technology and determined compassion to repair my broken body, and give me the opportunity to live again—Dr. Dean Elliott. Without God and Dr. Elliott, I would not be here today. Secondly, I would like to acknowledge my dear friend Audrey for growing with me on the ice rink, and being there for me first when I struggled to accept my diminished body, and now when I need an understanding ear.

I want to thank all those friends who encouraged me to write my story, and read the manuscript with glowing praise—Sharyn F., Nancy D., Lisa H., and Judy R. A special thanks is given to Gwen W. for the initial editing for grammar, punctuation, and phraseology. Most of all, I want thank my wonderful husband, Ray, for his many hours of typing and assembling the bits and pieces of my writings into some semblance of order. My story, my passion for life, and my rock in a world sometimes filled with uncertainty, is inspired by the enduring love of my husband.

Foreword

"If I can stop one heart from breaking, I shall not live in vain. / If I can ease one life the aching, or cool one pain, or help one fainting robin into its nest again / I shall not live in vain."
 –Emily Dickinson

These words may not have been spoken by Linda (Dale) Cook—or even been a part of her awareness—but they certainly define the person she is. Born the fourth and final child of an alcoholic father, and a mother who "pined" for the loss of her firstborn, Linda began searching for recognition at an early age.

Donald Dale lost his life at age two, when he caught his hand in the wringer of an early-model electric washing machine. It was the '30s, and penicillin was not available for stopping infections. Lenna Dale's life would be dominated by this loss, and the effects wrought on her view of living by the hardships of the Great Depression.

Leonard Dale suffered his own demons from the loss of his son, and sought solace in alcohol. But, Linda was his "Little Shit," and commanded a warm spot in his heart. By the age of 50, alcohol had ravaged his body and ended his life. It was just a few short months later when Linda's life would be altered forever.

This is Linda's story—a story of determination, of dedication, of the will to succeed, and of the desire to live one's life as an example for others.

—D. Raymond Cook

The Early Years

My first experiences on an ice rink were in our back yard at 607 E. Spruce Street, in Sault Sainte Marie, Michigan ("The Soo"). My dad loved to skate, so he would make a rink in the back yard as soon as we had enough snow. I was three years old when my dad felt it was time to put skates on me. My sister, Joyce, and brother, Ken, had already learned to skate, and finally it was now my turn. My dad carried me through the snow, to set me on the ice.

I couldn't stand up right away, but I kept getting up every time I fell. I refused to let anyone help me. My ankles were too weak, so my mother would wind tape around them each time I wanted to skate. Eventually my ankles would strengthen. First, I learned to walk on the ice with my skates on, and then it wasn't long before I learned to move my feet more in a gliding motion. I knew from the minute I had my first experience on the ice, I had fallen in love with skating.

When I was four, I joined the Hiawatha Skating Club at the ice rink in the Pullar Stadium. In my first ice show, I was a penguin. I felt so special! The night of the ice show, I managed to stay on my feet and even do a little spin. From the beginning, skating felt so right for me. Time passed, and each year I was improving more and more. When I was about eight years old, my mother decided I was showing enough interest to start taking lessons. Before I knew it, I was helping the skating teacher to give group lessons for other kids. I did this without pay, because I so enjoyed showing others how to skate.

I began testing at the first opportunity, and this involved spending more time on the ice, preparing for each level of testing.

LINDA (DALE) COOK

As the years went by, I became more confident in myself, and passed enough tests to earn a solo in the annual ice show. My personality was such that I drove myself to stand out from the other skaters. I wanted to do something just a little different from the others, in my solo routine. I kept working on a spin called the broken leg spin. I didn't see any other skaters using it, and when it came time for the show, I felt I could do it. Once I hit the ice, it went off without a flaw. This was the first time the hometown crowd saw one of their own doing a broken leg spin!

Playing with the Next-Door Neighbor/ Earning Money

As far back as I can remember, I enjoyed playing with my dolls and pretending to live in a home with them. I would sweep, dust, iron and take care of my baby dolls. I had a great imagination and made full use of it. This became my favorite pastime since television was not yet heard of, and we could only listen to the radio during certain times of the day. The adult philosophy was that children were to be seen but not heard. So I would go upstairs and move into my own little world of playing house. In looking back at this time in my life, this helped me a lot to imagine how things should look. I would listen over and over to music and imagine skating to it, picturing where to insert jumps and spins, or just perform some footwork.

A person's imagination can be used in positive ways. My dolls and my make-believe formed a learning experience. With my house playing, I had a little broom and an iron with an ironing board, which I often used. I learned to iron at a very early age because I always wanted my dolls to look groomed.

My best friend, Warren Erickson, lived right next door. We spent a lot of time together playing outside, and in his house. We started kindergarten together, walking hand in hand. His father walked us across the street to the sidewalk leading to the bridge over the power canal, and on to Garfield Elementary at the other side. I was so glad I had someone to walk to school with. It was very scary walking across the bridge. It was constructed of heavy steel girders that arched into the air, from one side of the canal to the other. Steel railings as tall as I was protected the edge of the walkway. The walkway on the bridge was made of wooden planks, some of which had big holes in them where they had rotted through. As a little girl, the holes looked very big, and I was afraid of falling into the rushing water below.

One day we were playing in Warren's house while his mother was ironing. I must have looked interested in what she was doing, because she asked me if I would like to give it a try. I said yes, and afterward she thought I had done a nice job. So, she asked me if I would like to do a little ironing for her for a dollar a basket. I was so excited to think I could actually earn some money! Of course, my ironing just consisted of hankies, towels and easier clothing to iron. But, the big thing was that I was actually earning money! Sometime later, when a new baby arrived at the Erickson household, she would pay me to push him in the buggy. As he got older, and I was now eight, she allowed me to watch him while she was busy in the house doing other things. I was proud that she trusted me, and I felt good about doing these household tasks so well.

Warren and me, September 1950
First day of school, kindergarten at Garfield Elementary

Dancing in Canada

I was only eight years old, and I went skating as usual on a Saturday morning. One of my girlfriends approached me and told me about a lady from Canada who was going to start coming over to teach tap, ballet and acrobatics. This really interested me, as I always enjoyed watching people tap dance. Right away I knew that I just had to go to the American Legion the following Saturday, and take lessons! I was positive that I was going, I just had to figure out how I was going to pay for the lessons.

When the big day arrived, I got dressed, took my babysitting money that I had been saving up, and walked to the American Legion to begin my lessons. It was such an exciting event for me, and I made sure I was there early. Luckily, my friend's mother was there, and she let me sit in her car until the doors opened. That was the beginning of my nine-year stretch of dancing lessons.

Within a few months, the dance teacher, Trixie Hardy, had moved her dance classes back to Canada. Now I had to somehow convince my mother that I could ride the ferryboat across the river, then walk about eight blocks to where the dance studio was located. This was quite an undertaking for someone so young. Our winters could get cold and windy, and the streets would be covered with snow and ice. Never once did I consider the hardships, or think about what could happen to a young girl traveling this distance by herself. My mother finally relented, so off I went with a little suitcase that I had claimed from a closet. Inside were my tutu, tap shoes and ballet slippers—I was very proud and happy!

A TALENT LOST/A LIFE WITH A PURPOSE

I would walk to the ferry by myself, pay the fare at the window in the wood-frame building, and go through the metal turnstile. Then it was a short walk in the harsh elements to the ferryboat, where a low metal railing separated passengers from the vehicles, and marked the path to the stairway to access the passenger cabin. Inside, there were wooden slat benches to sit on. The cabin surrounded an enclosed stairway that led to an upper level where the pilothouse was located. Often, the captain would see me approaching the stairway to the passenger cabin, and thinking that I was pretty young to be on the ferry alone, he would invite me to ride in the pilothouse until we got to the dock on the other side of the St. Mary's River. He also made sure I got off the ferry okay. I felt safer knowing that he was watching out for me, especially since I knew that he was a friend of cousin Shirley from Echo Bay, Ontario.

While I was working on the various tests in dancing, I got to perform for teas, recitals, and for a local live talent show called the Black Outs, held at the Ritchie Auditorium at the Sault High School. This was a fun show in which you had to audition for a spot on the program, and I always managed to get chosen. I progressed my way up through the dance tests, and finally earned my gold medal in dancing. Trixie decided that I should perform on a Canadian kiddies show on CJIC television. The station broadcast only in black and white, and was the first and only television station our area had available. The technicians would play a vinyl record, and I would perform the dance routines that I had been practicing. This was not my bag—by this time I was a teenager! I let Trixie know that if she continued to schedule me for live TV performances, I would have to quit dance altogether. I'm sure she didn't believe me, because I so enjoyed the sword dance, the Highland Fling, and even playing the maracas for Spanish numbers. I was just having fun with everything. But, my teacher kept putting me on TV, and after one such performance, I just left and never returned to the dance studio.

All the dancing lessons were not in vain, however, as they were very instrumental in developing poise and form for my skating. In dancing, a person learns to be graceful and how to listen to the beat of different types of music. This could be very helpful in designing and planning routines for the annual ice shows at the Pullar Stadium. I did teach some dance classes for a short period of time. Unfortunately, it became too difficult to find enough time for everything I was involved in.

The Bumstead Family

My mother came from a family of ten children. There were eight boys and two girls. Her last name was Bumstead. One of the most popular newspaper cartoons of the time was Blondie and Dagwood (Bumstead). You can imagine all the teasing and jokes that were made about that name! Some of my fondest memories were when everyone gathered at the Bumstead farm once a month for Sunday supper. When everyone was there, the head count was usually 30 to 35 people. These were days of laughter and lots of fun. My grandmother raised chickens, mainly for their eggs, and for eating.

The day was centered on catching about four or five chickens, whereupon one of my uncles would cut off their heads! Then the women would begin to pluck the chicken feathers, and prepare them for the meal. This may sound cruel, but one of the rituals would be to watch the chickens run around after their heads were severed. This made me sad until someone explained to me that the chicken was actually dead, and it was just the nervous system making them act this way. It wasn't long before I joined along with the laughter.

Everyone brought a dish to pass for supper. After the chickens were boiled to perfection, we all gathered around four or five tables, and began to feast on a wonderful meal. These family meals were a time when everyone was happy, and there were no sad faces or raised voices. It felt wonderful hearing the laughter, and listening to all the family stories. After everything was cleaned up, everyone headed back to their own home. The ride back to town to our house was a time filled with contentment. Arriving home after dark, it was time for bed, and fond memories of the day spent on the Bumstead farm.

My Own Bedroom

Our house on Spruce Street was very small for a family of five. My parents were renting, and it seemed that we made the best of it, as I do have fond memories of my surroundings. But, being the youngest, I was the one that didn't have a bedroom of my own. In fact, I slept in a baby crib in my mom and dad's bedroom until I was nine years old! In the spring of the year following my ninth birthday, my dad began construction on a new house for us on Maple Street. It was a very nice four-bedroom home, and I was to get my very own bedroom. I wasn't sure if I would get a real bed or not, as I was still sleeping in my baby crib, with the railing down so that I could climb in and out. I didn't ask—I thought that getting my own bedroom would be reward enough!

We moved in before the house was even finished, but it sure was an improvement over our old rental house. My mother found a roll-away bed for me to sleep on—I guess she decided that it was time to get me out of my crib. So, I slept in the upstairs hallway, as the finish work on my own bedroom progressed. Finally my bedroom was almost finished, and I was just happy to sleep on the roll-away in my very own bedroom. But, I got another wonderful surprise. My uncle called and asked if my mother and I could come over to his house. When we got there, I found out that he had a wonderful surprise for me. Uncle Leonard Bumstead had just bought his daughter a new bed and dresser, then she got married and moved out, and he wanted to know if I would like to have the set. The bed and dresser were just beautiful! He said this could be my graduation present when I finished high school. I was so happy, and felt that my new bedroom was now complete. No more crib for me! I can't believe I slept in it as long as I did. I adjusted well to my new home and the quiet neighborhood around us. This would be my home from 1955 when we moved in, until I got married in 1965. I had lots of babysitting jobs nearby, and the woman next door asked me to iron her clothes, too. That fall I started Sault Junior High School, and kept busy with my skating.

Summers on Calaboogie Road

When I was growing up, I usually spent most of each summer on a farm in Canada.

My Aunt Pearl and Uncle Bill Larocque owned and operated a dairy farm on Calaboogie Road, just past Echo Bay, Ontario, Canada. They were a family with lots of love and affection to share. I was very aware of their caring ways, as it was a stark contrast to the lack of warm affection in my own home. When I was about ten, Uncle Bill asked me if I would like to drive the John Deere tractor in the fields at haying time. This would leave more hands to load the hay from the fields, onto the hay wagon, using pitchforks. I was thrilled with the idea of actually driving a tractor. Up to this point, I had only done chores around the house, and small chores in the barn. Being young and inexperienced with machinery did result in some mistakes. Once, when driving the tractor down a ravine in the hay field, I didn't realize that the tractor should be in a lower gear. As the tractor picked up speed going downhill, the farmers were running faster and faster, trying to throw the hay on to the wagon behind the tractor! Finally the tractor jackknifed, and most of the load ended up back on the ground. No one said a cross word, they simply reloaded the hay wagon, and I continued to drive the tractor back to the barn. This incident was a topic for laughter for many years!

Rising time on the farm was 5 a.m. This didn't bother me one bit. I would get up, go downstairs, and sit by the stove to keep warm while "chomping at the bit" to get on with the daily activities. I just loved everything about these surroundings. After

LINDA (DALE) COOK

a hearty breakfast of eggs, toast from homemade bread, and a glass of fresh cold milk, the daily farm chores began. The days were long and hot, but I enjoyed every minute! Somebody actually cared about what I was doing, and often told me how well I had done. On Saturday nights, we would clean up, and everyone would gather at the Laird Township Hall for food, square dancing, and story telling. I was having so much fun that sometimes I had a hard time believing it was happening to me.

Occasionally, my brother, Ken, would come to stay at the farm for a few weeks during the summer. I enjoyed having him there to share my experiences. We sometimes tried silly things like riding on the backs of the cows. I recall one incident where Ken decided to lift up his tee shirt and touch the electric wire that marks the field for the cows, with his belly. After all, we were told not to "touch" the electric wire, so putting your belly on it should be okay. I'm sure he just wanted to show how brave he was, by taking the electric shock.

I hated to see each summer on the farm come to an end, but I knew skating would soon be starting for the winter, and nothing could keep me away from the ice rink. I spent my summers this way until I was about 13. I only wish every kid could experience this wonderful way of life on a farm. There is so much more to being right in the middle of daily farm life, than anyone can imagine. I thank the Lord for giving me the opportunity to be a part of such a wonderful life experience. I will always cherish this part of my life, and I believe it helped to make me who I am today.

Chapleau, Ontario

"The greatest accomplishment is not in never falling, but in rising again after you fall."
—Vince Lombardi

One very cold winter, I was asked to skate in Chapleau, Ontario. They were having an ice show, and asked us to participate in putting on a special program. I was excited to be invited to skate way up in Canada, where they didn't even have a road that went that far north. The only means of access at that time was by train. I imagined having so much fun, until I found out that the ice arena didn't have any heat, and they had real ice versus the mechanically made ice that I was used to skating on. Also, I hadn't thought to bring a costume that was made for warmth. All I had packed was a skating costume my mother had made me, tights, and of course, the mittens I was wearing. When we arrived, it was 50 below zero, and there had been a big fight on the ice the night before we arrived. We were told that they couldn't wash the blood off the rink, so we were to just try to skate around it.

I was determined to make the best of the situation, as we were to be a highlight of this special show. Unfortunately, everything seemed to go wrong. First, the record that I had chosen to skate along with would not make a sound due to the extreme cold. So, I began my number without any music. Then, it was so cold that my eyes kept filling up with water, and I had trouble seeing where I was on the ice. Yep, as you might guess, I skated through the blood! And yes, it caused me to fall! I was so embarrassed, but I got up and skated the rest of my routine, and everyone seemed appreciative. Looking back, this was a very good experience for me. I was proud to be a part of an ice show for a new audience, and it reinforced my determination to pick myself up when I fall, and continue to give it my all. The warm and friendly folks of Chapleau gave us a big party after the show to thank us for our performance.

Green Bay, Wisconsin

When I was 13 and 14, I had the opportunity to skate in Green Bay, Wisconsin, during the summer breaks from school. The Pullar Stadium in the Sault would remove their ice for the summer, so this allowed me to skate for at least part of the break. My friend Audrey Bailey and I were so excited to have a chance to skate under some very good coaches. The first year we stayed for a couple of weeks in a motel, not very far from the arena. The arena was new, and was located next to the field where the Green Bay Packers practiced for the summer. The first time we were on the ice was magical. It is hard to express the wonderful feeling I had. I didn't think of myself as a great skater, but I knew I had some potential. But, when I looked around at some of the other skaters, I was impressed at how advanced they were. At first they intimidated me, but it inspired me to work even harder each day.

As the days went by and I had several lessons (from a drop-dead gorgeous coach!), I started to feel more relaxed. Our usual day started at seven in the morning and ended around four in the afternoon. All of these hours on the ice resulted in very sore feet and lots of blisters! We could leave the ice for our lunch break, so Audrey and I would go and watch the Green Bay Packers football practice. I didn't know it at the time, but the world-famous coach, Vince Lombardi, led the Packers. The team was destined to become Super Bowl champions, and the most winning team in professional football history. I didn't know anything about football. The players looked like old men, and standing at the edge of the field, they just looked like sweaty athletes to me. One of the players approached me and asked if I would like to try on his helmet. I didn't realize that would have been an honor, something to be proud of. In looking back, I think he must have been insulted, as I told him "no thank you." I did tell him we were on a short lunch break, and had to return to the rink. When it was time to go home, we had mixed emotions. Our feet were pretty sore, yet we were having fun learning new skating techniques.

When we returned for the second summer, Audrey and I felt more comfortable about our surroundings. We stayed at a home that housed skaters. We knew this was going to be fun. Green Bay was a very nice town. We did a lot of skating and took lessons from the same pro that we had the year before. Audrey and I were both going to take our 5th Level test at the end of our training. I remember being so nervous when I saw the judges wearing hats with little whiskbrooms in them. I had never seen this before, and I was imagining what on earth they might be going to do with the whiskbrooms. All my fears came true. After we took our test, the judge got down on her hands and knees, and proceeded to go around all of the circles we made on the ice, to be sure we were always riding on the correct edge of the blade. At this point I knew in my heart that there was no way I was going to pass this test. I had let myself down, and, most of all, I knew I was in for trouble from my mother. Yes, I did feel bad, and yes my mother was furious at me. All I could think of was that I would take the test again, and pass it with flying colors. That winter I retook my skating test and passed it without any trouble. I will never forget this skating experience, and to this day I am so glad to have had the opportunity to skate in Green Bay, Wisconsin.

A TALENT LOST/A LIFE WITH A PURPOSE

Audrey Bailey and Linda Dale

Being a Majorette

I was always interested in anything that would give me a challenge. When I would go to a parade, I was fascinated by the performance of the majorettes. I was amazed at how they could manage to twirl a baton and walk at the same time. When I was about nine, I decided to ask for a baton as an Easter present. I was thrilled when I saw my shiny new baton, and immediately practiced over and over again, until I had learned a routine. I continued to watch parades, and practice the only twirl I knew.

When I was in the ninth grade, I learned that Sault High was having tryouts for majorettes. I found out when those tryouts were, and went to the high school. I desperately wanted to be a majorette, but I was worried about knowing only one twirl. When I got to the tryouts, I explained my situation and told them I could learn any twirl if someone would demonstrate it for me. I'm sure there were some who thought I was just bragging. The instructor demonstrated three or four new twirls that I could practice. I never doubted for a minute that I could learn the twirls I needed to get into the majorettes. I practiced for hours. I had only one week to learn these twirls, and I had to be able to do them with grace and speed. I was determined to be a majorette no matter what it took. At the end of the week, I went back to the high school with confidence that I had mastered everything that they told me to do with the baton. Needless to say everyone was surprised I could learn all this in one week. What they didn't realize is how stubborn I was when I decided I wanted to do something!

At last I was a majorette. I enjoyed leading parades, and participating in routines at halftime during football and basketball games. I got to wear the big hat and the wonderful uniform, and of course, the majorette boots. I truly loved every minute of it. I felt good about my accomplishments. However, there was something that bothered me. My parents never made an effort to see me perform, or lead a parade. I think this was one of the reasons I felt I had to succeed at everything I attempted. I was always trying to win their love.

When I Met Ray

It was the month of September, 1961, and I was at school having lunch with my girlfriends. One of my friends started talking about this guy named Ray Cook, and asked if any of us knew him. I said that I knew a Ray Cook when I was about six years old. This Ray lived across the street from me, and one summer he was hit by a car and thrown up into my driveway. I remember him being unconscious and taken away to the hospital. He was lucky to end up with just a concussion. I related that I had always thought of him as being a real mean kid. My girlfriend said this couldn't be the same guy. This Ray Cook was quite bashful, and really nice. The next day she pointed him out to me when we were in the hall on our way to another class. I remember thinking "Wow! He sure is cute!" The next time we girls were together, they bet me that I couldn't get a date with him within one week. As you probably have learned by now, I couldn't resist a challenge.

So, I began following Ray around at school whenever the opportunity came up, until he noticed me. I never spoke; I just wanted him to be aware that I existed. The following weekend there was a Halloween dance at school. I decided to dress up like a clown, go to the dance and have fun. I was standing in the gym listening to the music and enjoying fast dancing with my girlfriends. All of a sudden, Ray came up behind me and asked me to dance. He was so handsome, and very tall! I felt so secure in his arms. He noticed me all right. We danced every dance until the dance was over, and then he walked me home.

Ray was such a gentleman, it was hard for me to believe that he was the same Ray Cook I knew when I was younger. When we got to my house he just gave me a little kiss on the cheek, and asked me if he could call me the next day. I just floated into the house, and couldn't wait to tell my friends that I was quite sure I had a date with him. What I didn't realize was that this was the man I was going to marry someday. The most wonderful thing about him was that he liked me for who I was, not for what I had accomplished in skating, or anything else. We dated all through the school year. I felt I had found somebody that really loved me. He was my knight in shining armor, he didn't drink or smoke, and he had a steady job at the Red Owl supermarket. Ray was the perfect guy I had been wishing for.

Snow Festival Queen Candidate

It was a Saturday in late November, and I was busy doing my chores around the house. I knew it was almost noon, and I should start to get ready to go skating. Saturdays were always busy days for me. When I got to the rink the first thing I had to do was to teach group lessons, and then I had private lessons scheduled for the rest of the day. This wasn't just any ordinary Saturday, however. The club was going to vote on which member they wanted to sponsor as a queen candidate for the Soo Winter Carnival. The winter carnival was a big festival in Sault Ste. Marie. The whole town participated in all the activities. It was a fun time for everyone to get out and enjoy some winter fun.

This was the first year our skating club chose to sponsor someone as a candidate for Winter Carnival queen. I decided that when I arrived at the rink, I wouldn't participate in the selection process. I had never been chosen to run for queen of anything, and I didn't want to think that I might have even a slight chance to win. I knew the odds were against me, because there were about 300 members who could cast a vote for the candidate of their liking. I went about doing my job, and I noticed all the little whispers that were going on about the voting, but I didn't let it interfere with the job I was doing.

As the day was drawing to a close, I thought to myself, "Should I dare to get excited about the possibility of winning?" Then all of a sudden they announced on the loudspeakers for everyone to meet in the middle of the ice. The votes were tallied, and it was unanimous—I was selected to represent the skating club as the winter festival queen candidate! I could hardly believe what I was hearing, but yet was saddened for the other candidates that wanted the position themselves. Fortunately, joy overshadowed any sad thoughts I might have had at the moment. I felt like just going outside and screaming: "I'm the one they chose!" I felt so proud to think that everyone liked me enough to vote for me. It was a very warm, fuzzy feeling. I can remember just saying thank you, over and over again. I wanted everyone to know just how much I appreciated this honor.

By December, everything was getting really busy. The other skating "pro" and I were busy planning a Christmas show, and I was getting letters about different teas and banquets I was supposed to attend with senior classmates. In the middle of all this, my mother got a call from my father, who was working in Detroit. He was thinking about coming home for Christmas, but was sick and asked if we could travel there instead. I didn't see how I could, as I had made so many commitments. So I begged him to come home. He did, but when he got home he looked very sick. I thought he just needed some rest, and Christmas would cheer him up.

Dad made it through Christmas, but then decided he had better see a doctor. The doctor put him right in the hospital to run tests. I was so busy, and never for a minute did I think that he was sick enough to die. But three days after Christmas, my father passed away. That was such a shock to me, and I felt so guilty that I hadn't made more of an effort to visit him when he was in the hospital. On top of everything else my mother told me it was my fault that my father had died, because I had asked that he come home. That was a big burden to carry around, and I could not get it out of my mind.

As the days went by I stayed busy with school, skating and attending the various functions for all the winter queen candidates. The festival queen was to be announced at halftime of

Friday night's basketball game. My mother reminded me that she does her shopping on Friday night, so she wouldn't be there—and Ray had to work. So, I borrowed Ray's car, drove myself to the high school, and found the room where all the candidates were getting ready. I didn't let this dampen my spirits, I just proceeded to get dressed, and the other mothers were great in helping me with anything I needed.

Now it was time to go and make our appearance. I stopped and looked around the gym. Everyone had somebody there to care about her. I felt sad for a moment, but I just kept thinking of Ray waiting for me to pick him up after he got off work. I knew when I got into his arms everything would be perfect. I was selected as the Hiawathaland Skating Club queen candidate for the Soo Winter Festival—but I came in second in the competition, and that was just fine too. I knew I was Ray's queen no matter what the outcome was. I really don't remember anyone asking me if I was chosen as the festival queen when I got home, but I figured that was just the way things were.

The Night of the Accident

It was Friday, February 29, 1963. I was in Pop Wright's American Problems class. It was fifth hour—almost time to go skating. Several kids were talking about going to a district basketball game where Sault High was playing Petoskey, in Petoskey. It sounded like fun to me, since I had never been to an "away" game. Five of my fellow classmates were making plans for the drive to the Lower Peninsula. If I went, I would have to see if my skating students would take their lessons the next day. I thought long and hard about this, and I finally decided to try to change my pupils' lesson day to Saturday. So, I told the kids that were going to the game, if I could make the right arrangements, pick me up at my house at 5 p.m. I went skating and asked my pupils if they would agree to change their lessons to the next day. To my great surprise, they all said yes. I was home free. Now I had to hurry and get ready for the trip to the basketball game in Petoskey. I knew it was a bad time to be taking time off from skating, because another instructor and me were putting together the annual ice show for the end of March. But, I decided that to go away for just the evening wouldn't interfere too much. After all, I would be back the following day in lots of time to be at the rink by 1 p.m. Little did I know that my life was about to be changed forever.

We had a great trip to Petoskey. There were six of us—three boys and three girls—in a 1961 Chevrolet that belonged to the mother of one of the boys. I had a blast, and the fact that Sault High won the game, made it just that much more exciting. After the game we went to the Petoskey High School dance, and that was even more fun. We were all rather tired and hungry after all this excitement, so we decided to stop and have a hamburger and fries. I had only fries, because I was still too excited to eat.

For the ride home, the three guys said they would ride in the back seat, with us three girls in the front. We were all just good friends, headed home after a full night of good times. It was hot in the car, so I rested my face against the window and closed my eyes, knowing that I had a very busy day ahead of me on Saturday. I not only had my regular students to teach skating but I had to squeeze in four other kids from Friday's schedule.

We left Petoskey in darkness, with snow banks along the streets, and patches of ice on the roadway. I was just getting comfortable when I was startled by a loud scream. I quickly looked over at the driver. She had thrown her hands in the air, completely letting go of the wheel, and the car was out of control! I remember being tossed around, and then there was nothing.

News accounts of the accident and conversations with witnesses and my classmates were all that I had to fill in the accident details. I knew that the driver had lost control and failed to navigate a fairly sharp curve. Apparently, the car failed to make the S curve, and got wrapped around a big steel pole that marked a railroad crossing. The side I was sitting on was the side that hit the pole, and the car and I just kind of got wrapped together around the pole. I had been sitting on the passenger side of the vehicle, with another girl sitting between the driver and me. The side that I was sitting on received the full impact, as the careening automobile hit the pole. A couple of passing motorists stopped to investigate shortly after the accident. We were very lucky, because two of the people who stopped were a nurse and an off-duty telephone line technician. The technician was able to climb a telephone pole and hook up a phone to the wires. The man called an ambulance, and the nurse started to get everyone out of the car as quickly as possible.

A TALENT LOST/A LIFE WITH A PURPOSE

I learned later that after the first ambulance arrived, and as the kids started to get in the ambulance, one of the guys noticed I was not with them. They assured him there was no one else in the car. However, he kept insisting I had to still be in there. So, the nurse went back for a better look, and sure enough she found me mangled up under the dash. They called for an emergency crew to bring the Jaws of Life. When my body was finally extracted, a second ambulance had arrived to transport me to Northern Michigan Hospital.

My next recollection was when I was in the emergency room—I could hear in the distance, somebody talking about this young girl who is almost dead, and there isn't much hope for her. I thought at the time, "Who are they talking about, anyway?" It never registered that it was me, but I remember feeling sorry for the girl that was dying. Then I realized I couldn't move and I thought I saw blood dripping from my face. It all seemed very confusing to me as I fell unconscious again.

I really don't remember very much about the next few days or weeks, except that all my family was standing around me crying, and I couldn't figure out why. I couldn't see very well, and I was confused about what was going on. I wanted to let everyone know I could see him or her, and I wanted to ask them why they were crying. Try as I might, I couldn't communicate with them, and suddenly I would fall back to sleep.

When I was sleeping, it seemed like I never quit thinking. I saw Ray, my brother, my sister, and my mother and couldn't figure it out. Ray was in Chicago, my brother was in Washington, D.C., and my sister lived in Marshall. Why were they all here together? At one point, I felt myself drifting down a tunnel toward a light, and saw my dad with his hand reaching out to me. I knew he had died a couple of months ago, and I wasn't ready to be with him just yet. I kept saying, "No, Dad, I can't come yet." The light was warm and beckoning, and there was a beautiful garden of bright yellow flowers. Then it seemed like I was entering my body again. I guess I just wasn't ready to leave this precious world.

Then came the struggle to come out of the coma. At first I thought I was in a coffin, because my bed had a canopy over my head to keep the air I was breathing moist. I later learned that there also were many tubes in me, just to keep me alive. I had a "trachea" (a surgical hole in my throat) to let me breathe, and tubes in my nose to feed me, because my veins had collapsed, eliminating the ability to use intravenous feeding. I was packed in ice to keep my body temperature down because my brain was swelling. They didn't want to have to operate on me to relieve the pressure, because I was too weak to survive such a procedure.

My eyes were pushed out of their sockets, especially the left one, keeping my eyelids from completely closing. Both of my eardrums were broken, so I couldn't hear very well. I was paralyzed, so I couldn't move. I was in pretty bad shape. But, from the outset, my determination drove me to survive.

I had "round the clock" nurses and they liked to move me around frequently. I can remember thinking, if only they would just leave me alone. I recall that the baby formula they gave me through my nose was very filling! I would wake up each day for just a few minutes, and Ray would always be there. I couldn't see or hear him, but I could feel the fuzzy sweater I had given him for Christmas with my right fingers, and I knew he was there. I just had to let him know that I wouldn't always be like this, and I wanted to ask him to please wait for me to get better. I couldn't figure out how to let everyone know I was okay.

One night a nurse was leaning over my bed and I felt a pen or pencil in her pocket. She tried to keep me from moving around but I managed to knock it out of her pocket. The next day she told the doctor of the trouble I gave her the night before. He said the next time Linda wakes up, give her paper and a pencil and see what she does with it. The very next time I woke up, she gave me paper and

A TALENT LOST/A LIFE WITH A PURPOSE

a pencil, and I scribbled: take me for a Pepsi. Then I would fall back to sleep. This went on every day—I would wake up, and I would write a different little note. They soon realized I wasn't a vegetable and started to try to wake me up for good. They played a lot of music, and the song I woke up to was "I Saw Linda Yesterday," which was a popular rock and roll song at the time.

How is my dad how come he never come to much my

give me narrow
take me
for ride

I just
          I just know

              I just

be like this
me not not   the rest
                of my life
    of my life

Recovery

I remember I started moving my right foot to the beat of the song—that caused everyone in the room to realize that I was coming out of the coma. This was a very confusing time for me, because when you're in a coma, time doesn't mean anything. One day just leads into the next day. I remember an incident where they called the doctor over the intercom, and he came in and talked to me. I can't remember what he said, but it must have been in response to my awakening. Dr. Elliott ended up being a hero to me, and he treated me with an intense interest and a caring attitude. I had never been to a doctor before this accident. I never had any illness that required seeing a doctor before now. I feel so fortunate that Dr. Elliott was my doctor. I could feel his strength and determination to help me survive.

Waking up presented new problems for me. How do I communicate with anyone? I couldn't talk because of my trachea, and I was still almost completely paralyzed. I decided that using my eyes was the best way I had to try to tell people, "Hey, I'm here!" Then the questions started, as the nurses and doctors tried to find out just how much I knew. It was plain for me to see that this wasn't going to quit overnight. They would say my name, and ask if I knew where I was, over and over and over again. This went on for a few days, and finally I got strong enough to give them some dirty looks when I had enough! Then my right hand began to get some strength in it, and I tried to let them know I'm all right! I let them know that I knew what they were saying, by writing a few things on paper.

LINDA (DALE) COOK

They finally took the feeding tube out of my nose, and that sure felt a lot better. There were a few days (probably many days) that I just drew a blank. For weeks, they kept my temperature down by keeping me packed in ice, almost frozen, and big fans blew cold air on me 24 hours a day. This was a new procedure that had been tried experimentally elsewhere, with excellent results. I was aware enough to realize that they were taking the feeding tube out of my nose. Next, they thought that it might be time to sit me upright. I thought this would be a piece of cake, but I was surprised when I couldn't even sit up! I fell over every time they would sit me in an upright position. This led to an attempt to put me in a wheelchair, but they forgot to tie my arms down. My arm caught in the spokes of the chair, and because I didn't have any feeling in my arms, I couldn't tell where my arms were hanging, so over I went, chair and all! This also caused a big commotion.

Once I was upright in the chair, I was on my way again. They took me down to the nursery to see a new baby that weighed only one pound. I was so glad to just be out of bed. But, I couldn't believe how tired it made me, just getting up. After seeing the baby, I remembered dreaming about the little baby they had shown me. Apparently they had been telling me about this baby before I completely woke up. One of the next steps in my therapy was for the staff to bring a TV in my room for me to watch. When they brought it in, I didn't want to tell them I couldn't hear it, because I didn't want to hurt anyone's feelings. So, I pretended everything was just fine, even though I couldn't hear it, or see it very well.

I began daily visits to the x-ray room, and the doctors decided to wire my jaws shut because they had been broken in four places. My nose and pelvis were also broken. But, because of lying still for so long they were healing by themselves. The wires in my jaws were designed to hold my upper and lower plates together, so that the jawbones could mend. There was a small opening in the front, where I could only suck liquids. By this time, I'm sure that my weight was declining, and they were just trying to give me as much nourishment as possible.

One day my mother brought my senior picture into the room and said to the doctor, "This is what Linda really looks like."

Up to this point, I had never seen a mirror, so I wasn't sure what I looked like. I began to think I must look pretty bad, because of what my mother said, and I was aware that people stared at me all the time. The girl in the next room had a broken leg—one day she came into my room and I asked her if I could see her mirror. She had no idea I had never seen myself, so she went and got her mirror. When I took a look at myself, I couldn't believe what I saw. I looked like something out of a monster movie! I threw the mirror across the room without thinking about the fact that it didn't belong to me.

I felt very depressed after seeing what I looked like. So, the doctor thought it might be better for me to have a roommate. He saw that I was moved to a semi-private room. It was nice having someone else in my room, but she was able to eat real food, and she liked to have the curtains open. I was starving for food by this time, and the sunlight gave me pains in my head. I accepted the fact that these were just more challenges I had to deal with. Again, after reviewing the many x-rays, the doctor felt that my skull wasn't healing very well. The solution was to put a real tight elastic bandage around my head, which gave me an extreme amount of pain. All in all, I felt terrible most of the time.

One thing that kept me going, was the letters from Ray, and the visits he would make to see me when he could. The nurses would read them to me as they arrived. I also received flowers and cards every day from the skating club, and all my friends back home. I missed the ice show, and another person took my place in putting part of the show together, and teaching all my students. I was so thankful that everyone seemed to help with my unfinished work. I wondered how I could ever show people how much I appreciated everything they were doing for me. Then I decided I better concentrate on getting better first. It seemed that every time I turned around they were finding something else wrong with me.

Next, I began physical therapy. This was very degrading to an 18-year-old, because I had always been independent, and able to do things on my own. But, for everything they wanted me to do, I would work twice as hard as they had asked me to. One thing they would do was put roller skates on my limbs to move them back and forth on a table or floor, trying to build back some muscle in my legs and arms. I also had to learn to crawl on my hands and knees. I was so embarrassed, but I thought if this is what it takes, I'll do it. For small muscle coordination, I would practice putting small objects in a jar with my hands, which was also very embarrassing for me.

Again, the many x-rays led to the discovery that I would have to have surgery on my little toe. They had put a metal pin in my toe, so that slowed down the physical therapy for a while. Now I was really getting depressed. By this time, I was aware that some of my classmates came to visit me, and they passed out when they took one look at me. Of course, that just made me think that my looks would scare anybody. I was getting very insecure, worrying that Ray might leave me because of my looks, and it was taking me longer to get better than I thought it would. But, he kept on writing me, and coming to see me when he could. He would say, every time he left, that he wanted me to be able to complete a task that I couldn't yet complete. This gave me the incentive to try to succeed in whatever he had wanted me to attempt. I wanted to please him, so I would try very hard to accomplish the goal he set for me.

I was getting so tired of having to be waited on for everything. I started to try to do too much, and ended up in trouble most of the time. I remember one time I wanted to go to the bathroom instead of using a bedpan. After all, the bathroom was so close and I would have things to hang on to. So, I tried, and just as you would imagine, I fell to the floor and couldn't get up. I was furious with myself! Another time, I remember I wanted to change the station on the TV. So, I wiggled down to the bottom of the bed, and started to reach out. This time, I fell hanging over the bottom of the bed. Now I really figured I was in trouble, wondering how I was ever going to be able to function normally. I felt bad for a while, and then I decided self-pity just wasn't going to get me anywhere.

I can recall that on the sixth or seventh week in the hospital after the accident, I was staying awake more and more during the day, and it appeared to the doctors that just maybe I was going to be able to lead somewhat of a "normal" life. They decided to start trying to explain to me what my limits would be. The doctors felt that my being completely normal was never going to happen. Over a period of a week, I was told that I would never be able to have children, I would never walk again, and that I would never see right or hear very well. My mind was a blur trying to imagine what this was going to be like. Another day, the doctors would discuss all my fractured bones. I was told that these were not a priority in the beginning, because they didn't think I would live very long, and they were just concentrating on keeping me alive. So now I learned that I had two broken feet, ten broken toes, fractures in both shoulders, a broken nose, jaws broken in four places, pierced eardrums, a broken pelvis, and cracked ribs. If this wasn't enough, my skull was fractured, and wasn't healing real well. On top of that, they said I might never have any feeling in my left side. This kind of bothered me because it felt like my body was split right down the middle. I tried to rationalize all of this, and was sad for a while. But then I decided they couldn't be talking about me, because I was getting better, and that was just the way it was going to be.

I finally got the wire out of my toe, and the wires out of my jaws. In the place of wires, they put thick rubber bands on my jaws, and I still had to suck liquids through my clenched teeth. By this time, I weighed just 65 pounds and looked like a living skeleton. It had been two months since I had been outside, and more than 30 days of the past 60 were in an unconscious state. I was really getting anxious to get home because it was my senior year in high school. Never once did the thought cross my mind that I wouldn't graduate with my class. I was the drum majorette of the school, and I realized that I would have to give up my position, but I wasn't going to let this stand in my way of getting better. Even though it was so hard for me to accept, I realized that I just couldn't be a majorette again.

Going Home

The day finally came when the doctor said that the best thing for me to do now is to go home and keep up the physical therapy. The other pro from the skating club, Joan Atkins, came with my mother to take me home. She brought her station wagon and put a chaise lounge lawn chair in the back so that I could lie down. When it was time to leave the hospital, they wanted to wheel me out in a wheelchair. I wouldn't get in it; I wanted no part of that! I was determined that I would never get in another wheelchair, even if I had to crawl. So finally they gave in, and said okay. My mother got on one side on me, and the nurse got on the other, and I staggered out of the hospital. But, I was proud of the fact that I didn't get in a wheelchair. Joan gave me a white orchid to wear for my trip home. I can't tell you how excited I was! On our way home, we stopped to see a huge crucifix with Jesus on it. At this time, I thanked the Lord for giving me another chance to live.

The cross was beautiful and what a special time to see it. This had been the longest time I had been out of bed for a long time. I looked forward to the rest of the trip home—Petoskey is about one and half hours from Sault Ste. Marie. I was getting tired, but was just too excited to sleep. Finally we arrived home—and now the task was to get me into the house! I just took hold of my mother and Joan, and held on real tight while staggering into the house.

Once I was in the house, I wanted to see my bedroom. My mother had painted it my favorite color, lavender. It looked beautiful to me. I was happy to finally be able to sleep in my own bed. This meant that no nurses would be coming in to check on me every time there was a shift change. This was almost too good to be true! When I looked around my bedroom, one of the first things I noticed were the many jars of money sitting on the floor. They were big jars with a label on the front of them that read "Donations for Linda Dale." I felt overwhelmed once again, to think people really cared about me. That night felt so good to sleep in a big bed, my own bed. As everyone knows, hospital beds aren't very wide, and just don't seem very personal. Everything now seemed perfect.

I soon learned that two ice shows were held in my honor, and that the hockey league also put on two benefit games for me as well. All proceeds from the events were for me. This made me feel very humble. I couldn't imagine all this was done just for me. I felt the giving nature of people, and was overcome with gratitude.

My first night home went just great. The next morning my mother went to work and my aunt came to stay with me during the day. There were no nurses to give me breakfast, or to help me with my hair. Now there were new challenges waiting for me. My aunt prepared my breakfast, but doing my hair with my one usable hand was almost impossible. My aunt saw me trying to fix my hair, and asked if she could help. So I let her help me. You can imagine how it felt not being able to do my own hair. Once again I told myself this is only temporary. On this, my first day back home, I could hardly wait to get the day in motion. The day itself went real well, but I always seemed to be falling asleep. This made me realize just how weak I was.

My mother still wasn't convinced that I didn't need a wheelchair. But I told her if she got one, I wasn't going to get in it. I felt if I got in a wheelchair, I might never get out of one. That just wasn't in my plans. My secret plan was to use a walker for a few days, and then try to walk, and get back in school. Even though the doctor advised me against going back to school this year, I was determined to graduate with the rest of my class. The class had put on an amateur show on my behalf, and gave me the proceeds. I felt that the least I could do was to show them how much it meant to me to have my class help me out.

My mother finally relented and got me a walker. I used it for several days, and then decided it was time to try to walk on my own again. Try as I might, I just couldn't manage by myself. One day one of the majorettes came to the house to get my uniform. I knew it was hard for her to come and get it, so I let on as though it didn't bother me. In reality I felt like somebody had just stabbed me in the heart. I was so upset! I somehow kept my feelings to myself. It wasn't too hard because I could no longer cry. My tear ducts had been damaged in the car accident, and to this day I cannot form tears.

The girls I chummed around with would come once in a while, and talk about getting ready for whatever they were going to do that evening. They thought this would cheer me up. Instead it really made me feel bad because I couldn't go with them. Although it was very thoughtful of them to stop by, I could hardly bear to see them leave without me.

I let a little doubt creep into my mind wondering if I was ever going to be normal. I prayed to the Lord to please just let me be like everyone else, and please do something about my face and eye. At this time, I still had one eye that was completely turned in to the corner. This made it very difficult to see correctly when I had both of my eyes open.

But I was supposed to wait for at least six months to see if the eye would correct itself. If it didn't, doctors would try more surgery to correct the eye.

I wanted to go to school, and nothing was going to change my mind. So my mother informed the school I was going to come back. I was to alternate days, going only half days—one day in the morning, and the next day in the afternoon. I still could only manage staying awake for two hours at one time—then I would start to fall asleep wherever I was. The school seemed to be very helpful in regard to my problem. They would let me have a study class in between each class. I thought, "Boy, now everything is going to be all right." But then we got a call from the school saying I couldn't go to school because they weren't equipped for handicapped students like myself. Little did they know, I didn't consider myself handicapped—just slowed down temporarily! Anyhow, making the school see my point of view was going to be a problem. Luckily the president of the school board, Maurice Strahl, was on my side. He told them they couldn't keep me out if I managed to get around. My classmates heard of all the problems they were giving me, and they took it upon themselves to take turns giving me rides to school, and helping me from class to class.

I sure was grateful for all the support my friends were giving me. When I finally settled into the school routine, I had no idea how hard it would be for me to let all my peers see me look so terrible. Of course they didn't know what to say to me either. So a friend would often help me to my desk, and I was so embarrassed by the way I looked, I would put my head down on the desk. Needless to say that didn't make it any easier for the kids to talk to me. The bell would ring and someone would come and get me. I was hanging on to a crutch with one arm, and hanging on to my classmate with the other. What a sight I must have looked like staggering down the hall! I never noticed anyone staring at me, thank the Lord for that. Next it was time for me to go to the study room for a rest—then the procedure of getting me to another room would start all over again. Classes were difficult because I had missed over two months of school. I had so much homework to catch up on, and tests to take. It was overwhelming.

At the end of each day, at about 3 p.m., I would go to the hospital for physical therapy. Trying to learn to walk was tougher than I ever imagined it could be. Because, after all, I not only could walk before, but I could skate, tap dance, do ballet, gymnastics, march in parades and sword dance. How could just plain old walking be so tough? Believe me, it was. I still didn't have feeling on the left side of my body. I guess the brain gives signals to parts of the body telling it when to move, and I had injured over half of my brain, so that meant teaching my brain how to do things over. After all that, I would go home and sleep for a while, then try to do some of my homework with a patch covering my left eye.

At the same time all this was going on I began to realize how thin I was. But my jaws were not healed enough for me to eat solid foods yet. Anyhow, being thin was the least of my worries. In the evenings different people would come over to take a look at me. They meant well, but I felt like a freak at a sideshow.

Sault High was having the annual awards show. I was asked to sit on stage with some other kids that I knew were receiving an award. But, I wondered why I was asked to sit with them. I couldn't figure out what I would get an award for, because I had missed so much school. I sat there very excited about being on stage in front of everyone, but wondering why I was there. Suddenly, they announced my name. I knew I couldn't walk up there to get whatever they were giving me. Then the presenter came to me with a trophy, and announced that I was getting the Majorette Trophy. This trophy was so big, and it shined like a diamond! It was so big that I couldn't hold it. It was to go back in the trophy case with the rest of our trophies with my name on it— what a surprise! Of course this made my day just perfect. I was so happy that words could not begin to describe what was in my heart. I could hardly wait to tell everyone at home and of course, write to Ray, who was working in Chicago, and tell him all about my wonderful day.

As the days went by, with my routine staying the same, it was getting closer to graduation and I had a bundle of work yet to do.

A TALENT LOST/A LIFE WITH A PURPOSE

I knew that I could never get it done in time to graduate with my class. I was beginning to think that all my hard work was for nothing. Then, my teachers said they would let me graduate with my class, but I would have to go to school for a couple of weeks after graduation. This was music to my ears. I tried to attend some of the banquets and teas they had for seniors, but most of it was a blank to me.

The day finally came when we were to graduate. I was very excited, but scared too, because I still couldn't walk unassisted. As I was helped down the aisle of Ritchie Auditorium, I saw the stairs I had to go up to get on the stage to receive my diploma.

The boy behind me helped me up the stairs. All of a sudden the president of the school board, Maurice Strahl, came to the microphone and announced my name, and started to tell my story. This was unusual because the principal, Sam Dubow, was the one who had been handing out the diplomas, but Mr. Strahl seemed to have mine in his hand. When he got done talking, everyone stood up and applauded for me. At this moment, I knew that I was walking across that stage to receive my diploma without any assistance! The boy behind me went to help me, and I told him I was okay. I was going to walk by myself to show everyone who had believed in me, that I wouldn't let them down. But, after making it to the podium and accepting my diploma, when I got to the other side of the stage, I saw stairs that I had to somehow navigate down. I looked at the crowd and they were still clapping, so I asked God to please take me down those stairs. He did, and I just seemed to float down the stairs. Happiness just filled my heart, thinking that all these people really cared about me, and that I had walked across this stage in spite of all the odds.

Everyone was talking about the senior prom. The big question was whether I dared to think of being able to go? I decided that wild horses couldn't keep me from going to the dance I had been dreaming about for the past four years. My mother got busy making me the most beautiful dress you could ever imagine. It was lavender, and just too pretty to try to describe. There was a little problem though—Ray was still working in Chicago, and his boss told him if he left to go see me anymore, he could forget coming back to work for him. I felt really selfish, but I just had to go to this dance. I had worked so hard to look a little bit normal, so that I would fit in and not be stared at. So I called Ray and let him know how important this dance was to me. Of course, he said he would be there, even if he lost his job. The night of the dance came, and he looked so handsome I couldn't believe he actually wanted to have anything to do with broken old me. I felt like a million dollars in the formal dress that my mother worked so very hard to make perfect. Ray put a lavender orchid corsage on me, completing my fairy-tale look. I felt beautiful for the first time in a very long time.

We went to the dance with Ray hanging on to me so very tight, so as not to let me fall. When we arrived at the high school gymnasium, the music, the decorations, and the special lighting were all fabulous... I was caught up in the moment and the atmosphere. I was having fun—something I didn't think existed for me anymore. We danced and danced, with Ray holding me so close to him, I could stand and dance just like everyone else. He smelled so good, and I felt so secure in his arms that I didn't want the night to ever end. When they announced the last dance, and Ray looked at me with love in his eyes, I felt like we were the only two people on the floor. The dance had come to an end, but our evening was still not over. We were going out to Ray's niece's cabin for a party. She was also a fellow classmate. I went home to change, and to tell my mother I was going to a cabin with four other couples. She was worried that I might get too tired, and begged me not to go. But, being the stubborn person that I was, I went anyway. I knew that I would be safe in Ray's arms.

When we got to the party, everyone else had already arrived. There was plenty of laughter and jokes, and a lot of good food. It was everything I hoped it would be. I started to feel really tired, and Ray sensed how exhausted I must be. We went and lay down on a couch, and the last thing I can remember was his strong arms holding me, and how secure I felt once more. I fell fast asleep, while the other kids continued their party. I slept through everything that was going on around me. It didn't matter, as I was right where I wanted to be—in Ray's arms. When I woke up, it was morning, and I knew my mother was going to be furious with me for not coming home sooner. She would probably blame Ray for keeping me out. This wasn't Ray's idea, it was mine—and I'm so glad he allowed me to be like everyone else. This whole evening was better medicine for me than a month's worth of therapy.

Ray lost his job. I was glad, on one hand, knowing I would able to see him more often now. But now he had to find a job in the Soo. It wouldn't be easy to find a job, because at that time there were not too many jobs available for someone our age. He looked and applied everywhere, but never heard back from any employers. Without my knowledge, he went down and signed up with the U.S. Navy. I think his parents thought this would be good for him, because he had been so worried about me. Maybe they were right, it was good for him but I was devastated. I thought, how could I ever go on without him? He was my strength and my reason for living. He would be so far away that I wouldn't be able to see him for months at a time. This was going to be one of the hardest things I had to come to grips with. I just kept telling myself everything would be okay.

Challenges

Again, I had to concentrate on walking. By this time, I could walk, but I would stagger and bump into things. If you didn't know me, you would think I was drunk. All my friends were getting summer jobs and preparing to go to college in the fall. Once again, I felt so alone. I wasn't well enough to get a job, and I couldn't see well enough to go to college in the fall. Mr. Strahl had told my mother that he would personally see to it that I would have a scholarship to the Michigan College of Mining and Technology, Sault Branch, if I ever decided to go to college. In the back of my mind, I thought that I had my skating to look forward to this winter, determined that I was going to be able to skate again. I thought, how can I do this? My therapy just wasn't going fast enough to suit me. I thought of a plan, and it was time to begin my plan.

During this period of time, my mother was working at our county building. The county building was over halfway to town, and she always parked her car in the parking lot across the street from where she worked, which fit into my plan perfectly. My plan was to try to follow the crack on the side of the sidewalk, to help keep me from staggering so much, and when I got to my mother's car, I would get in it and rest so that I could make it the rest of the way uptown. When I got uptown I planned to go into a dime store, and sit at the restaurant counter and have a pop. Then, I would retrace my steps, and I would end up back home. This seemed to work quite well. I did this every day, trying to build up my strength. The clerk at the dime store got to know that I was coming, and would have a nice cold pop waiting for me. The only thing that really bothered me about sitting in the restaurant was that there was a mirror right across from where I had to sit. I looked at my ugly face every day, and tried to keep my head down so people wouldn't stare at me. I didn't realize some people thought I was drunk because of my inability to walk correctly. There were constant whispers, and the fingers pointing in my direction.

I eventually quit walking uptown, and my family thought it might be better for me to get away for a while. There also were rumors circulating that all the kids in the car on the night of the accident had been drunk. This was so far from the truth. I was 18, and never had a drink in my life. My father was an alcoholic, and I saw what it did to a family. I was really against drinking or smoking. Not only that, but I was a true athlete! It was time I got some relief from all the stares and gossip. My sister, Joyce, lived in Marshall, Michigan, which was about five hours south of the Soo, and no one knew me there. She invited me to come and stay with her and her family.

Before I decided what I was going to do, I had another wonderful surprise. My brother came home from the Navy to help out my mother and me. It sure was nice to see him, but I also felt bad knowing that I was the reason he had to come home. He was enjoying being in the Navy, and living in Washington, D.C. His duty assignment was to chauffeur high-ranking officers and officials. He loved it, and now he had to give it up to come home. My mother got him an early release because she didn't have much money, and Dad had just died two months before my car accident. She needed some moral support too, I think. It was great having him home. He never complained, and never said a word to me about being disappointed about having to come home. He just got a job and gave Mom his paychecks. Not many guys his age would do that. He was twenty years old and should have been able to start a life of his own. Instead, he was giving a sister help, and providing financially for the household. I felt deep thanks for my brother, and for his love and support. I will never forget how much he sacrificed for me.

My Summer in Marshall, and at Big Star Lake

My thoughts now turned to making some decisions about what to do this summer. Inside, I knew what I must do to keep my sanity. I needed to go to my sister's and get away from all the stares and whispers. So I told my mother what I had decided to do, and she agreed that would be the best thing for me at this time. I can't remember how I got to my sister's house, but she welcomed me with open arms. It was a great next step for me. Joyce and Gerald Hamilton had two children—a little boy, Ricky, and a girl named Cheryl. I adored both of them. They lived in a mobile home, and it was a little crowded, but she made me feel welcome, and never said anything about me being in the way. It was fun being with little kids that needed me to help them, instead of having to have someone always helping me. I could go outside without anyone staring at me, or hear anyone whispering something about me.

While I was at my sister's house, a guy asked me to go out with him just as friends. I was so lonesome for Ray; I thought why not go? I might enjoy myself. We decided to go on a picnic with my sister and her family. Everything was going well until we went swimming, and it was even harder walking in the water. He didn't realize I hadn't been swimming since the car accident. I was too embarrassed to say anything to him, and the water was getting deeper and deeper, and I couldn't swim—I began to panic, but somehow I got back into shallow water. This was enough swimming for me. I had been a very good swimmer, but because of my left side being paralyzed I just couldn't manage to swim. We got out of the water, had our picnic with my sister and her family, and it was time to go home. I will never forget what he said on our way home. He looked at me and said, "I sure wouldn't want to be you when you get old, you are going to have arthritis so bad." At first it hurt my feelings, then I thought what does he know? That was the last time I saw him.

I was enjoying my stay with my sister but my cousin called and asked me to come and stay with her for a while. I didn't want to leave my sister, but my cousin was almost the same age as me, and she had two younger sisters. We always had so much fun together. I was hoping we still could. My sister took me to their house in Detroit, which was a couple of hours away. This was the first time they had seen me since the accident, so I wasn't sure how everyone would react to me. I was so surprised; they treated me like I was the same old me! I was so happy, I was sure I would have a great time being there. Once I got settled in, my aunt and uncle explained they both had to work, and it would be up to us to keep the house running smoothly. We also had some little chores to do--this was okay with me! My aunt treated me just like one of her own kids. Every day we did something different. We laughed all the time, and my cousin and I told each other silly little things that teenage girls would talk about. Gosh, this was great, especially the laughing part. I hadn't had too many things to laugh about in a while. It was like being in television's *Leave It To Beaver* family. Everyone got along and my aunt and uncle never fought. They lived like people I had only seen on TV.

The weeks went by, and I would receive letters daily from Ray. He was in Navy boot camp. Boy, did I ever miss him. He had not only been my boyfriend for the last four years, he was also my best friend. When I would get really lonesome, I would imagine being in his big strong arms, and once again feeling secure. I felt there was nothing life could throw at me that with him by my side, I couldn't conquer. I always had a reality check, and attempted to make the best out of a difficult situation. My cousins and I were still having fun, but it was growing near to the time when I would have to go home. I hated the thought of having to face what lay ahead for me at home. My aunt came home from work one day and asked us if we would like to go to another uncle's cottage on Big Star Lake near Baldwin, Michigan. This was wonderful; I would have one last fling of pure enjoyment before heading home.

We all loaded ourselves into my uncle's car for the trip to the lake. When we got there, the cottage I had imagined in my head was more like a mansion. We all piled out of the car and started choosing which bedroom we were going to sleep in. My cousin and I, of course, slept in the same bedroom. We were becoming inseparable. We still laughed a lot, and told each other crazy little stories. The car accident was never mentioned. My extended little family acted like it never happened. It was exactly what the doctor would have ordered for me for the summer, I thought. A few days went by, and my mother and brother came to the cabin. Then everyone else started to arrive. My mother's family was having a small family reunion. It was nice seeing everyone, but kind of sad, too, because this meant I would be leaving with my mother and brother soon, to go home.

What lay ahead was very uncertain for me. There were questions that I asked myself over and over, only to come up with unclear answers. I knew one thing for sure; there was still a lot of work ahead of me if I was going to continue to recover completely. I also knew I had to keep a positive attitude, not only for my own good, but if I expected people to treat me normally, I had to act like I felt normal. The question I had to ask myself was, am I prepared to put on the biggest act of my life? The answer could only be, of course, I would do whatever it would take.

The day came when we would have to say our good-byes. My brother, mother and I got into the car for our long trip north. On our way home I had time to think about everything that had happened to me in just the last six months. My body was crushed in a car accident in March, and I graduated with my high school class in June. I then managed to have a great summer with relatives. I said to myself, "You sure have come a long way!" If I could do all this in the last six months, just think what I could do in the next six months!

Home, Attempting to Skate Again, and Getting a Job

Riding in a car for any distance made me a little bit nervous. This was something I would have to work on. When I got home everything looked the same, except I noticed that all the jars of money were gone from my bedroom. It kind of surprised me, because I thought they were meant for me. I didn't question anyone about it, because I figured my mother just put them away.

Two days later my mother suggested it was time for me to try and get a job. I couldn't believe what I was hearing, but she was dead serious! It wasn't that I didn't want to get a job. But I thought no one would hire somebody who couldn't walk or see right. Also, I was too embarrassed to go to people and ask for a job the way I looked. I was hoping to get my old job back as skating instructor, even if I couldn't skate; I still had the knowledge of how everything was supposed to be done. I figured I had a month on the ice before the skating club started for the season. I was sure I would be able to at least skate in a line. To my surprise, my lawyer began calling and telling me I had better quit trying to get better, because it wouldn't look too good in court if I didn't appear to be completely handicapped. I didn't say anything to him, but I would never quit trying to get better. After all, a court hearing could be several years away.

At the same time, members of the board of directors of the skating club started to call me. They would always start by saying they would love to have me back as an instructor, but they wanted me to retake all tests again. I couldn't believe what I was hearing! After all, I wasn't brain dead; I just had some physical problems to overcome. To comply with their request it would mean taking all six tests over in front of a group of women that never even skated. In the first place, they must have known I couldn't take these tests now—the tests required a lot of very precise movements and balance that most people don't ever accomplish in their lifetime. I had trained hard for years for each and every one of these tests. Just one test could take the whole winter to pass. Boy, what a slap in the face! I knew better than to argue with these women, so I just said they had better get another pro. Once more my heart was broken. How could they do this to me? As I hung up the phone, I felt so angry. I felt like the skating club had let me down, at a time when I could use their support the most. I decided to just wait for a few days to see what would happen.

Sure enough the president of the skating club called me back—it wasn't that they were changing their minds, they just offered me some ice time to try help me get back on my feet again. My first thought was to tell them off. Then I realized that I really could use this to my own advantage. I knew that having the ice to myself would be a big help, because I could avoid people staring at me. So I politely told them thank you, this would be great. I told them to call me when all the arrangements were made—which I knew would take a few weeks. I thought this would give me time to get myself together. In the meantime, my mother was still after me to get a job. I thought there was no use in trying to make her understand how I felt. So I decided to go uptown to all the stores and fill out applications.

One day I got up and tried to look the best I could. I began my journey of walking uptown in search of a job. This was no easy task because I still couldn't walk without staggering, and the further I had to walk, the worse I would get because my left leg, which had no feeling, would tend to get tired quicker than my right leg. The walk uptown was at least ten blocks from where I lived. When I reached the uptown area, I decided to go up one side and down the other side, and go in any store that would need sales clerks. So I did, and of course every employer I met would stare at me and immediately say he wasn't looking for any help right now. This really destroyed any self-esteem I may have had left. It made me very angry with my mother for making me do this. After making all the rounds, I had to begin my journey home. I was dead tired and still had ten blocks yet to walk. All the way home I thought about how disappointed my mother was going to be in me. My mother got home shortly after I did. When I told her nobody was hiring, she wasn't mad, she just suggested that I keep looking. I didn't say anything to her, but was thinking to myself—it will be a while before I go out on the streets looking for work again.

It was about a week before skating started and I was anxious to get my skates on. Before the car accident I had bought a pair of new custom-made skates with special toe picks on them for jumps. I had only worn them about three times before the big wreck. The day finally came when skating started, and no one had called me to tell me when I was supposed to skate. I decided to go down to the rink, and hoped my old friends would be glad to see me. I didn't think about all the kids that had left for college though, and a lot of my friends weren't there. Thank goodness my best friend, Audrey, was still there. She lived just one block away from our first home. Audrey was my classmate in school, and had skated in the club just as long as I had. She came and met me at the doorway, and we found a bench where we could put on our skates together. I remember how difficult it was tying my skates, because I couldn't use my left hand very well. When I first stood up my ankle started to turn over, but I thought everything would be okay when I got on the ice.

I went to step on the ice, and I grabbed the side of the boards that surrounded the rink. I was embarrassed, scared, and surprised that I couldn't even glide on my skates. I had been skating since I was three, and now I couldn't even glide on the ice! At this, I said, "Please, Lord, let me skate." I waited for a few minutes and tried again. This time I started to stand on my own. God must have been listening to me, I thought. Then I went to put my left foot on the ice and my ankle turned right over. I didn't let this keep me from trying over and over again. I was so busy trying to skate, I hadn't noticed all the people watching me. When I did, it really bothered me because I figured they were probably saying, "Poor Linda, she used to be a pretty good skater—but look at her now."

At that moment, I headed for the entry, to where I could take my skates off and just get away from all the stares.

I still wasn't completely discouraged. I thought with a little practice, I just might be able to skate again. Also, if I could get some kind of brace for my ankle, it would help a lot. A few days passed and I was notified that I had the whole rink to use exclusively, or so I thought! When I got to the rink there were people from the skating club sitting on the bleachers, ready to watch me skate. If only I could just skate out onto the ice and show every one of them that I was just fine. But I did a reality check and knew that wasn't likely to happen today. I put my skates on and went on the ice, and of course it was very difficult for me just to stay on my feet. I figured out that if I just pushed with my left foot I could glide a short distance. So I began to skate around the ice very slowly. I felt like screaming: "Hey, am I doing all right yet?" But I didn't say anything and I thought it was time for the show to end, so I went and took off my skates. The funny thing was that nobody spoke to me, and it really hurt my feelings. This didn't stop me though; I was still determined I was going to be able to skate again.

I went back to the rink and did the same thing again and again, with an audience watching every move I made. The whispers were almost unbearable. I looked up in the bleachers and my heart was in my throat. I felt like shouting: "You won, everyone, you won!" I wasn't doing any better than on the day I started. I longed for someone to give me some support. I guess they didn't know what to say to me. I pledged from that point on, that if I ever saw anyone floundering through something, I would always give him or her a word of cheerful encouragement.

The time had come for me to make a decision that would affect the rest of my life. Was I never to smell the ice again, see the building itself, or feel the wind against my face as I skated to a song that I had picked for a solo performance? This wasn't really happening to me, was it? I realized that yes, it was. When I had fallen for the last time, I put my face to the ice and kissed it, as I knew this was the end. I put my head down, not wanting to see the people anymore, and did my best to skate to the opening that led to where I was to take my skates off for the last time. I sat on the bench alone and heartbroken. Couldn't anyone see how much pain I was in? I sat there for more than a half-hour, until I realized that it was time for me to take my skates off for the last time. So I did, and held my head up high and left the building, never to look back.

On my walk home, I gained some composure. I had to face my mother as if everything was okay. When I came in the house, she was making supper and Ken was home. I was glad for that, because he was always happy—maybe his good mood would make me feel better. If only Ray were here, he would know the right thing to say to make me believe that everything would be okay. But he was still in Navy boot camp in Illinois. Then I thought maybe he wouldn't understand how empty I felt inside, having to give up the most wonderful gift God had allowed me to use for so many years. When I went to bed that night I asked God why didn't He let me die when I had the chance to. Life wasn't going to be the same without being able to skate.

In the following weeks, all I could think of was the fact that I had failed at skating. Then Ray called and said he was coming home for a weekend. That sure lifted my spirits. I could hardly wait to see him, it seemed like it had been an awful long time since we were last together. I hoped that I had made enough progress for him to notice. Finally the day arrived for Ray to come home. When we met, our eyes locked on each other, and his big strong arms were around me, just like they were supposed to be. Everything in my body just melted, having him so close to me and being able to smell his shaving lotion. He was so handsome; my eyes never left him for a second. I was right; he knew exactly what to say to cheer me up. He was just what the doctor ordered. It was getting harder and harder to watch him leave, when it was time for him to return to duty. I was never sure when I would get to see him next, and I was getting so very lonesome for him. The day came when he left once again. I can't remember what we had talked about, but I knew I could not give up on myself, because he was counting on me getting better.

Working at War Memorial Hospital

I heard that the hospital was hiring nurse's aides. I knew this would make my mother happy, and it would give me something to concentrate on, other than myself. During the application process, I took a test and answered all the questions I could. I didn't think I would get the job, because I still looked rather scary. My eye was still turned in, and I still wasn't very steady on my feet. I thought that if I could get the job, I could start doing something nice for others, because I knew firsthand how people felt when they were sick. I got a call at home that I had the job. I couldn't believe it, but it was for real! The next day, I picked up the uniform that I was to wear. This was a miracle; somebody actually wanted me to work for them. I vowed never to let anyone down that believed in me. My first assignment was performing the duties of a clerk on the floor, handling the charts of each of the patients. Everyone treated me like I was just like one of them. For the first time since I had left my cousin's, I was being treated normally.

I had a responsible job, and I was good at it. Then, one day they were short of help on the floor, and asked if I could help. I jumped at the chance, because I was going to be able to work directly with the patients. I was sure this was where I could be the biggest help. I felt that I had so much love to give, and I had a desire to provide good care to each patient they assigned me. I loved my work. I had one elderly gentleman patient who seemed to respond to me more than the other hospital personnel. One day I wore a little yellow bow in the side of my hair, because he couldn't see very well. I thought he would know me from the other nurses if I had this little bow in my hair. The bow was only about two inches long, but bright yellow. The bow was a big hit with this gentleman, and he seemed to be having a better day than usual. I felt happy that I had put a smile on someone's face that day. Oddly enough, the head of all the nurses in the hospital called me to her office. I couldn't imagine why, except that maybe she found out how happy I had made this patient, because he was very sick and didn't have long to live. I got a real surprise, however, when she started to scold me for wearing the bow in my hair. She said it wasn't part of my uniform, and I was never to wear anything like that in my hair again.

Then she proceeded to tell me why she hired me in the first place. Apparently she felt no one was going to hire me looking like I did, so she took pity on me. That was the last thing I needed to hear, but I thanked her for giving me the job, and said I would leave the bow out of my hair. Again, I could have sat down and said "poor Linda," but I chose to make her feel bad that she ever said those words to me, by working just as hard as I possibly could. When I got back to the floor where I had been working, everyone wanted to know why I was called to the office. When I told the other personnel on duty what the director of nursing had to say to me, they all started to laugh. If you think about it, it was kind of funny. In my eyes the patient should be the first thing to think about—not whether or not a person is wearing a little bow in her hair! The next day, the gentleman said, "Hey, sunshine, where is your bow?" I just told him I couldn't wear it anymore, the supervisor reminded me that it wasn't part of my uniform. I had many wonderful experiences working in the hospital. Overall, I enjoyed it very much, and I received great satisfaction helping people.

Eye Surgery

I had gone to see an eye specialist a few months before I started to work at War Memorial Hospital. The doctor said that I would need an operation in order for my eye to straighten out, and enable me to see correctly. My mother was trying to see if the Crippled Children's Association would pay for the operation. She finally heard back from them and they said they would pay for the entire bill. This was great news! This meant they could schedule me for the eye operation as soon as possible. In the meantime, I kept working every day. I went to work at 3 p.m., and got off at 11:30 p.m. I usually wasn't ready to go home and go to bed after work, because I slept most of the day, waiting to go to work. Nighttime was a bad time for me anyway. I really missed Ray, as he was now in Navy Service School in Great Lakes, Illinois.

After work, Audrey and I would sometimes go out to a little drive-in hamburger stand to have something to eat. We would ride around for a while, then she would take me home, where I would watch some TV and go to bed. I would turn the radio on and listen to Dick Biondi spin the latest rock 'n' roll records. The station was WLS, from Chicago, Illinois—they had all the popular hit songs of the time. When "Blue, Navy Blue" would come on, all I could think of was Ray. I would wish that I could fall asleep, so that I could quit thinking so much about what I was missing. But, daylight would eventually come, and I would start my routine all over again.

It had been about four weeks after I started working at War Memorial Hospital, that I received a letter telling me that my operation was scheduled for the following week. I was glad to be finally getting this procedure out of the way, but I was scared as well. Upon my visit with the doctor who was going to perform the surgery, he told me there wasn't any guarantee that this type of surgery would help me, and it was even possible that I may end up blind in my left eye. I thought about everything he said, and I made up my mind right then and there, that it was worth the risk. I didn't feel that I wanted to live the rest of my life not seeing right, if there was even a slight chance that my eye could be corrected. I reasoned that if I closed one eye, I could see better—so, if the surgery left me blind in the left eye, I would at least have one good eye.

The day finally arrived when I was to leave for Marquette General Hospital in Marquette, Michigan. My mother drove me there, and I got all signed in, and went to my room. The surgery was scheduled for the follow morning. That night I would hardly sleep—I was scared and felt so alone. The next morning came, and my mother hadn't arrived at the hospital in time to see me before they wheeled me into the operating room area. It seemed like I was lying outside the operating room forever! Apparently the surgery scheduled before mine was taking longer than they had planned. I lay there with all kinds of crazy things running through my head, wishing Ray was there to hold my hand and to assure me that everything was going to be all right. Then, I wished my mother would come and see me before I went into "the room." Finally I was wheeled in for surgery, and everything happened so fast that I didn't have to think about it any longer.

The next thing I remembered, I was in the recovery room with somebody trying to wake me. I thought, why don't they just go away, I'm finally getting a good sleep. But they were very persistent about waking me up. I felt myself being wheeled down a hallway, and I wondered where they were taking me. The nurses put me in bed, and the next thing I knew, they were bringing me a tray of food. That was about the last thing I wanted to see!

A TALENT LOST/A LIFE WITH A PURPOSE

My mother was now by my bedside, insisting that I should eat some food. It was fish, and it smelled terrible to me. I tried to eat it to make my mother happy, but it didn't stay with me very long before up it came! The tray was removed from my room. Within a couple of hours, my mother informed me that it was time for her to return home. Once again, I was alone, sick, and scared about what lay ahead. Next, a nurse came in and told me to lie flat on my back, do not get out of bed, and make sure not to roll over on the side that had the eye surgery. I thought, "Great, how am I going to make sure that I follow all these instructions, when all I wanted to do was go to sleep!" I felt so miserable and alone, and it seemed like everything hurt. I was sure that this had to be the worst experience I ever had to go through.

In the middle of the night, I had to go to the bathroom, and they never told me what to do about that! The halls were dark, and I didn't see any nurses go by my door. So, I thought there is only one thing to do—get out of bed and go to the bathroom myself! I got up very slowly, because I felt dizzy. I made it to the bathroom okay, and saw that there was a mirror right in front of me. I thought, "Do I dare take a peak at what my eye looks like?" I did, and then wished that I hadn't. My swollen face was a sight to behold. I got back into bed, but I couldn't go to sleep. It seemed like I lay there for a long time, waiting for daylight.

The light finally came peeping through the curtains. All of a sudden, it seemed, the whole hospital came alive. A tray of food was delivered to my room, and now I was hungry and ready to eat anything they gave me (except for that fish that I had tried to eat the day before!). I ate everything on my tray. There were several slips of paper on my tray that were menus for the following number of days that I was scheduled to be there. I filled them all out, not knowing I should have filled out just one at a time. So, at lunchtime, they brought several trays of food in to me. I didn't want to hurt anyone's feelings at this point, so I ate all the food!

LINDA (DALE) COOK

My left eye started to bother me a lot, so I rang for a nurse. She came in and checked things over, and rang for a doctor. The doctor removed the bandages, cleaned my eye, and bandaged me up again. I never received any feedback as to how things looked, or what to expect, as the doctor never said a word. Apparently he had very little bedside manner, as I had questions I wanted to ask, and I guess he just figured he was too busy to talk to me.

I lay in bed all day, and it was getting very boring not having anyone to talk to. I didn't know even one soul in this hospital, or in Marquette for that matter. Night finally came, and the same routine was followed the next day. I wished that Ray would call or even send me some flowers. My brother and his wife sent me the most beautiful bouquet of flowers. That cheered me up! Flowers always seem to make everything look a little brighter. The second full day after surgery seemed to pass very slowly as well. Night finally came, and I was able to get some restful sleep. The next morning, the doctor was supposed to take the bandage off my eye. I was sure that as soon as he took the bandage off, I would be able to see just fine. But, he came in, whipped the bandage off, and headed for the door without even speaking to me. I took one look around, and started to scream at the doctor to come back—I wanted to talk to him! At this point, I guess he knew that he better at least come to the door of my room to get me to stop screaming for him. He came back, but just to the doorway. I said, "Doctor, I don't see right. I see worse than I did before the surgery." The doctor told me that I would just have to give it time, and I would see just fine. I couldn't figure out how that could be. Luckily, a very kind nurse came into my room and explained to me that it would take my brain a few days to adjust, before I could see normally out of my left eye. It will seem like normal sight to me, but wouldn't to someone else trying to look through my eyes. It is amazing what the brain can do to re-route signals. Thank goodness for that nurse, but the eye doctor sure was no Dr. Elliott!

I had to stay in the hospital for two more days, so I called my mother in the Sault to let her know. Mom said she couldn't get away, and that I would have to take the bus. The next day, the doctor asked me if someone was going to come to take me home. When I told him I had to take a bus, the doctor said absolutely not! He felt that I was in no shape to try to navigate a bus ride on my own. I called my mother back, and she said she would try to arrange something. The next morning, when I was supposed to be released, my mother called to say that Audrey's mom would be coming to pick me up. Shortly after we hung up, Mrs. Bailey came in the room. I was glad to see someone I knew. She was so cheerful, and it made me feel really glad that she had come.

When I got home, everyone wanted to look at my big surgery. Almost all of my face was black and blue! I looked like I had been in a huge fight with somebody bigger than myself. I thought that I had better wait for a few days before I went back to work. I was hoping all the pretty colors on my face would disappear. The pretty colors did fade, so I went back to work. It felt good getting back to work, and to be surrounded by people. Now that I had my eye fixed, it looked almost normal. I was satisfied with the outcome of the surgery. Not only did I look better, but also I felt so much better about myself. I was ready to get started in helping someone else out—my assigned patients.

There was only one thing that was still bothering me. It was the fact that Ray hadn't even called or sent a card during my stay in Marquette. Even if he was busy, I felt that he could have taken a few minutes to give me a call. He knew that I was really scared to have this operation, and I would need his support. Being the insecure person that I was, I began to wonder if he still cared about me. I was going to wait for him to contact me first. After a few days, he called and said he was wondering why I wasn't sending him any letters. I explained to Ray where I had been. He thought that my surgery was scheduled for the following week. He felt really bad. So naturally, I told him I understood. Now everything was right between us once again. It was so hard being so far away from him, only hearing his voice every few weeks. Thanksgiving was just around the corner, and I hoped that Ray would be able to come home for a few days. It had been several months since I had seen him. I knew when he left boot camp he might be going even further away. I began to wonder how I would ever get through being separated from Ray.

I decided that I would "pour myself into my work," to take my mind off my worries. I offered to work for anybody that wanted a day off. I was now working six days a week, on a regular basis. It helped to keep busy. When I was busy, it not only helped me keep my mind off of Ray, but I also could put skating in the back of my mind. Never did I completely forget about skating, because I would dream almost every night that I was skating in an ice show. Not only was I skating, but I was able to complete a terrific performance, gliding through the program I had designed. I always silently hoped that I would once again be able to skate. I guess that my dreams and the routines that constantly played out in my head, kept the hope alive.

The winter was very bitter and cold. And, each day at work, my patients would present new challenges. One day I had a gentleman patient who was very ill. He was not expected to live much longer. As I was in his room caring for him, with the curtain pulled around his bed, he suddenly took his last breath. I quickly took his vitals, but there was no sign of life. I reported to the nurse's station right away, and asked for nurse confirmation. It was confirmed—the man had expired. The nurse immediately paged a doctor. In all the confusion, I hadn't noticed that the gentleman's wife was still sitting in a chair outside his room. Right away, I sat down beside her while we waited for the doctor. I couldn't tell her that her husband had died until the doctor made an official announcement. In the meantime, she began to tell me all the things that she and her husband were going to do as soon as he got better. The whole time I was listening to her, I felt so bad because I knew that none of this was possible now. It seemed to take the doctor forever to come. I thought, this is one of the hardest things I have had to do as a nurse's aide. The doctor finally came, and then sadly told the gentleman's wife the bad news. Boy, was I ever glad when this night ended.

One particular night, it was storming quite hard outside. I remember hoping that my car would start. I had bought my mother's 1956 four-door Desoto from her, as she purchased a newer vehicle. But, it didn't want to start when it was cold outside. As I went out to get in my car, I said a little prayer. Sure enough, this time it started for me. I sure was glad it started—this meant that I wouldn't have to bother my brother for help again. As usual, I went home and fell asleep listening to the radio.

It was nearly Thanksgiving, and Ray didn't think he could make it home. I was so disappointed. Then, just days before the holiday, he called and asked whether or not I could come down for Thanksgiving if he sent me a bus ticket to Chicago. We would have a big dinner at his sister's house in Mt. Prospect, and she would love to have me spend a few extra days with her and her family. She lived just a short distance from where Ray was attending the U.S. Navy Service School Command training. When I told my mother of my plans, she almost had a fit! She said that there was no way she would allow me to go. Apparently she had forgotten how stubborn I could be. Ray and I continued to make plans. Mrs. Bailey even gave me some extra spending money for my trip. I will never forget how grateful I felt for friends like Audrey, and her mother, Millie.

There was no way I could convince my mother that this was something I had to do. But, I think she finally realized it was out of her hands. That night, after packing and trying to decide what I should take with me, I went to bed but couldn't sleep very well, thinking about my trip in the morning. When I woke up, I was so excited to actually be able to see my honey by the end of the day! It was going to be a long ride on the bus. It would take 11 hours to get to Waukegan, Illinois. This is where I was to meet Ray. The bus left the Soo at about 6 a.m., and was scheduled to arrive in Waukegan at about 5 p.m..

The morning I boarded the bus, it was another bitter, cold day. I was hoping that the bus had a good heater. The bus was toasty warm, so I began looking around for someone interesting to visit with. We didn't have assigned seats, so I could sit anywhere. I found a nice old lady to sit with, and we introduced ourselves. The bus began to move. I was finally on my way to see Ray. The lady was friendly, and she had brought some snacks to eat on the trip. She shared her snacks with me. I thought that was nice of her. I never thought about bringing something on the bus to eat. Eating helped to pass the time. Also, the lady told me all about her family, where she was from, and what she had done when she was in the workforce. I certainly was glad I had someone nice to visit with.

We had driven quite a distance, and it was almost noon. The bus was supposed to stop for lunch in Milwaukee. Just as I was thinking that we must have been getting close to Milwaukee, the bus began to pull into a coffee shop. I wasn't really hungry, but I was glad just to get up and walk around. I decided that I had better have something to eat, because I didn't know how long it would take us to arrive in Waukegan. We ate, and everyone got back on the bus. We were on our way again. I learned that we were supposed to arrive in Waukegan at about 4 p.m. I felt certain that Ray would be waiting for me.

We finally arrived, and as everyone got off the bus, I started looking around to see if I could see Ray anywhere. I didn't see him, but I thought maybe he was in the bathroom, or was on his way to the bus station. So, I sat down inside the bus station and started to wait, expecting to be there only a few minutes. One hour went by, then another. Then, I started to get worried that I might be at the wrong bus station. Ray had given me a telephone number where he could be reached in an emergency. I thought that this was an emergency, so I called the number. No one answered the phone. Now I was really getting worried. There was nothing I could do but wait. There wasn't another bus leaving until the next day. I really had no intention of leaving without seeing Ray. There had to be a good reason why he wasn't here.

I waited another hour and was just getting ready to try to reach someone else. There were a lot of creepy-looking guys hanging around the bus station. I sure didn't want to be there after dark! All of a sudden I looked up, and in walked Ray. It was so good to see him. However, I was mad that he made me sit at the station waiting for him so long. Of course, he did have a good reason. He couldn't get "liberty" any sooner, and there was no way to let me know that he was going to be late. I didn't stay mad very long, now that I was with him.

We had to catch a train to his sister's house, and her husband picked us up at the train station. When we arrived at their house, all her family was waiting to see their Uncle Ray. His sister had six kids. Her house was beautiful, and even had two bathrooms! I had never been in a house with two bathrooms. So, that alone impressed me. Everyone was talking and laughing. I thought to myself, "Would I ever get some time alone with Ray?" There seemed to be so much commotion going on all the time in this big family. We all talked for a while, and it was getting late, so his sister showed me to where I was supposed to sleep. I was to sleep in her son's room, and he was going to sleep on the couch. Everyone went to bed, I kissed Ray goodnight, and drifted off to sleep. I was exhausted from the bus ride, and all the excitement of meeting everyone.

The next morning, I awoke to chatter coming from the kitchen. I went and freshened up in the bathroom, and joined everyone for breakfast. Boy, it sure took a lot of food to feed six children, and now four adults, in a private home setting. I felt a little out of place, but Ray and his sister made me feel welcome. It was nice being included in a large family. The plans were for Ray and me to take the train to downtown Chicago. This sounded like a fun adventure, and we would be off doing something by ourselves. Ray's sister let us borrow her car for the trip to the train station. When we arrived in Chicago, we found everything decorated for Christmas. The buildings were huge, and the streets seemed to be teeming with people in the holiday spirit. We went in several big department stores, right downtown. I remember thinking that if I ever let go of Ray's hand and got lost, I wouldn't even know how to get out of the store. There were so many doors on each of the buildings, each leading to a different street. In one store, we saw a display of beautiful silk scarves. Ray walked up to the counter, and turned to me and asked me to choose one. They were all so pretty, I couldn't decide, so Ray picked out a white one for me. I felt very special.

We arrived in Mt. Prospect in time for supper. Ray's sister, Jean, and her husband, Art, were going to a neighborhood party. They asked us to babysit the children. Naturally, we said yes. This wasn't my idea of a fun time, but Ray's sister had gone out of her way to let us be together for Thanksgiving. The next day was Thanksgiving, and the dinner Jean had prepared had so much food, I couldn't believe my eyes. Not only was there a large variety for the main course, but Ray's nieces had been making Christmas cookies for the past week. There was every kind of cookie that a person could imagine. I had a perfect Thanksgiving, being with Ray and his family, but I knew that the next day I would have to go home. After we cleaned up the kitchen after our big dinner, we sat around and talked. Before I knew it, it was time to go to bed. I kissed Ray goodnight, settled into bed, and once again fell fast asleep.

The morning came too soon, and I knew it meant having to leave. We got a ride to the train station, said our goodbyes, and Jean gave me a box of cookies to eat on my way home on the bus. Ray and I had to go down into a tunnel to get to the train we had to catch. But, when we got to the terminal, our train had just pulled away. This meant that we had missed our train, and we might miss the bus that I was supposed to take home.

Return from Waukegan

The next train finally came, and we got on. Now we were to begin the rest of our journey. It was fun riding on the train, but it was to be the last ride Ray and I would take together for a long time. We finally arrived in Waukegan, and hurried to the bus station. We had just missed the bus by a few minutes. Now what were we going to do? There wasn't another bus leaving for the Soo until the next day at noon. Ray had to be back on the base by midnight, so we knew he couldn't stay with me until the next day. He didn't want me to stay at the train station all night, because we didn't think that would be a very safe place to spend the night. As we began to walk, Ray had an idea—he thought we should look for a motel room for me to spend the night. I didn't like that idea, but I didn't have much of a choice. Another thing, neither of us had much money, and the only thing there was to eat was the box of cookies that his sister had given us. We walked for several blocks down the main street and saw a small motel. It was now about 5 p.m., and Ray had an hour until the last train would leave that could take him back to the base. We went into the office of the motel, and Ray told the clerk what happened to us. She said she had a room, and only charged us half of what it normally cost. As I entered the room, I began to get really scared to stay by myself. Ray spent the next hour assuring me everything would be okay. I still felt scared to death inside. It was time for Ray to leave, and I knew I didn't have any choice but to stay there. He again assured me everything would be all right, and kissed me goodbye. I was sure nothing would ever be right again.

A TALENT LOST/A LIFE WITH A PURPOSE

After Ray left, I just sat on the edge of the bed and felt very sorry for myself. I wondered how on earth was I ever going to manage without him. After just sitting there for about an hour, I realized I was hungry, remembering that I didn't have any supper. I sure wasn't going to go outside of the room looking for food! The only things I could eat were the cookies Ray's sister had given to me to eat on the bus. I started eating one cookie after another and soon I felt full. Boy, the cookies sure were tasty. I still couldn't go to sleep, so I watched some TV. After a while, my eyes started to get very heavy. I turned off the TV, trying not to think about the next day.

I woke up with a startle the next morning. I could hear a vacuum cleaner. I wasn't sure what time it was, and I was afraid I had missed the bus again. I got dressed real fast and got my suitcase and went to unlock the door. It wouldn't unlock. I tried everything and I couldn't get the door open. I started to panic—this couldn't be happening to me! I didn't know what to do, so I started to yell out hoping the cleaning lady would hear me. I began to think that somebody was playing some kind of sick trick on me. The cleaning lady heard me and came to see what was the matter. I explained to her I couldn't open the door, and she immediately unlocked it for me. She couldn't understand why I couldn't unlock the door myself. This was very puzzling for me as well. I thanked her, then picked up my suitcase and headed down the street.

I was trying to remember exactly how Ray had told me to get to the bus station. I just kept walking until I saw something familiar. Then I realized how hungry I was. I hadn't had anything to eat except cookies since the morning we left Ray's sister's house. I saw a little restaurant, and I decided to go in and get some toast and a glass of milk. My money was almost gone now, but I figured I could manage until I got home. I ate, then started on my way to the bus station again. My suitcase was getting heavy, and

I didn't know how much further I could carry it. Then I looked up, and the bus station was in plain sight. I felt so relieved when I knew I didn't have to go much further. When I arrived at the bus station, I looked at the clock and I had an hour before the bus left for Sault Sainte Marie. I went straight to the phone and called Ray. I was lucky I got through to him. I told him I was at the bus station and everything was all right. I didn't tell him about not being able to unlock my door, because I felt so stupid, and I didn't want him to worry any more than he had already. Then I called my mother and told her when my bus was leaving, so she would know when I would arrive in the Soo. I was hoping she could pick me up. But the bus was going to arrive in the Soo late, so she told me to take a taxi home. I hoped that I had enough money for a taxi.

It was now time to get on the bus. I stepped up to give the bus driver my ticket, and he said, "The bus is kind of cold today, so maybe you would rather sit near the front, because it is warmer at the front of the bus." I thought this sure was nice of him to try to make me feel more comfortable. So I sat right behind him, thinking this would be a comfortable place to sit. No one sat next to me, and I was kind of glad because I didn't feel like talking. The bus began to move down the highway, and before I knew it we were stopping for supper. I didn't think I had better spend any money because I wanted to have enough money for the taxi when I got in the Soo. I sat down and had a drink of water. I didn't mind, it felt good to stretch my legs for a few minutes before getting back on the bus.

Before long, it started to get dark. I thought I might be able to go to sleep without anyone looking at me. I was very self-conscious of people looking at me. The next thing I knew, the bus driver put his hand behind the back of his seat and was rubbing my leg! I thought maybe he was just stretching his arm, and accidentally hit my leg. I moved over in my seat closer to the window, so his hand couldn't accidentally hit my leg. To my surprise, he did it again. Now I was getting very uncomfortable, but I didn't want to make a scene. So I kept quiet, and every once in a while he would rub my leg. I could have just died. If this had happened today, I would have handled the situation quite differently. Being young and very innocent of the real world, I just kept quiet so that I wouldn't bother anyone.

Finally we arrived in the Soo. I quickly got off the bus and thanked God I was home where it was safe. I got a taxi and went home. Everyone was sleeping, so I went and got into my own bed and breathed a sigh of relief that today was over. Today and tonight were going to be a thing of the past, and I would never to tell my mother a thing about what had happened. Being in my own bed sure felt good. I was so tired that I fell right to sleep.

The next day I didn't get up until my mother had gone to work. I didn't have to be at work until 3 p.m. I lounged around and watched some TV. I kept thinking about everything Ray and I had done in Chicago, and how much fun we had. Everything else that happened didn't seem so bad now. At least I got to spend some time with Ray. When I got to work, it seemed like I had never left. My shift was over before I knew it. Now it was time to go home and see my mother. I got into my car, and went home to face all the questions that I knew my mother would ask. Before I went to sleep that night, I sat down and wrote Ray a long letter telling him all about my interesting trip home. I could even laugh about the trip now! I heard my brother coming home for the evening, and it was comforting to hear him acting happy, as usual.

The days flew by, and it was getting close to Christmas. There were Christmas decorations in all of the stores and the downtown was all decorated, too. I was anxiously waiting to hear if Ray was going to be able to come home for Christmas. Then one night, I got a call from Ray telling me he couldn't come home. He also told me he got his orders showing where he was going to be stationed next. I was hoping it would be close enough for me to see him once in a while. But instead, he told me he was going to be going to San Diego, California. This was so far from the Soo. As far as I was concerned, he may as well have told me he was going to Mars! I knew I wouldn't see him for a real long time. My heart was about to break, and there was nothing I could do about it. When I went to work, I told all my co-workers I would work any shift for them during the holidays. I didn't have any reason to celebrate Christmas. Maybe if I worked every day I could lose myself in my work. I was now working an average of six days a week. It did help me to keep my mind off of being so lonely. But, when I went home, I listened to the radio and wrote Ray letters, and ended up getting pretty sad anyway.

Christmas came and went, and nothing seemed to matter to me right now. I was aware that my brother had a girlfriend, and he seemed really happy with the relationship. He deserved some happiness in his life. I sure did envy him though; being able to hold the person he loved in his arms. One day just led into the next day, and I never seemed to do anything exciting. I would just go to work, come home and clean the house, and go to bed. I was glad I had Audrey to hang around with once in a while. We didn't do much but go to a movie or just get a hamburger. Sometimes we would just sit and talk for hours. If anyone could make me laugh, she could. I had my brother, my mother, my work and my girlfriend—but I always felt so alone.

Ray sent me a very pretty ring for Christmas, and he made sure he let me know the ring was called a friendship ring! The ring had three little diamonds in it, and it looked like an engagement ring. I felt very hurt that he called it a friendship ring, because we had been going together for four years. I was hoping for something other than a dinner ring—he could have called it an engagement ring, and I would have been perfectly happy! But he didn't. At first I put the ring away and wouldn't wear it. Then after a few days, I calmed down and decided to wear the ring to work. The first person that saw the ring on my finger congratulated me on my engagement. I had to tell the person it was just a friendship ring, and that made me feel even worse. Everyone who noticed the ring thought the same thing, that the ring was an engagement ring. I loved the ring, but I decided if Ray felt he didn't love me enough by now to want some kind of commitment, I wasn't going to wear the ring anymore. That night after work, I took the ring off and put it in the box it came in. I was tired of explaining to everyone that it was only a friendship ring.

Ken and Bonnie's Wedding

One night, while my mother and I were watching TV, my brother, Ken, came in the door with his girlfriend to announce their engagement. Bonnie showed us the ring that Ken had bought her. I was so happy for them, and knew that Bonnie would make a wonderful wife for my big brother. I must confess, though, I was very envious of her. Here I had been going out with Ray for about four years, and he sends me a friendship ring. On the other hand, my brother had only been going with Bonnie for half as long as I had been going with Ray. She gets the real thing, and I get a friendship ring. Ken and Bonnie were planning a summer wedding. I was really surprised that Bonnie asked me to be in the wedding ceremony. This was going to be so much fun. I was excited for them.

Ray and I kept writing to each other, and he would telephone every once in a while. The winter seemed to drag on forever. I routinely had problems starting my car when the weather was cold. I knew I could count on my brother to help me with my car, but after he was married, I would be on my own. I decided not to worry about that; I just wanted to get through the winter.

Summer was just around the corner, and we were planning a wedding shower for Ken's wife-to-be. Also, I had to look for a dress to wear in the wedding. I was told not to worry about anything too fancy, as his girlfriend was very easy to please. I told her how envious I was of her, and that I would probably have be wheeled down the aisle in a wheelchair, because I would be so old before Ray would marry me! We had a laugh about this. My mother and I had a big shower for Bonnie, and she got a lot of nice things. Bonnie looked so happy. I knew she was going to make my brother happy, and that was important to me. My sister, Joyce, and her husband, Gerald, with their kids, would all be at the wedding. Gerald was also going to be in the wedding party. I found a dress in my favorite color, pink. I showed it to Bonnie and she liked it. So the next day I went down town and bought the dress. Bonnie's sister was to be her matron of honor, and she thought the dress would look nice on her as well. Now all we had to find was some kind of headpiece to wear. I was going to leave that decision up to Bonnie. I didn't know anything about bridesmaid's headgear!

One day Bonnie called and said that she had found some cute headpieces that would go with the dresses we were going to wear in her wedding. We saw or heard from Bonnie frequently over the next few months. She was always baking something for Ken. He would bring whatever she gave him home, to share it with my mother and me. I remember one time she sent cupcakes with blue frosting on them. I thought this was really cool! I didn't bake much at this particular time. Any homemade baked goods we got sure tasted good.

Well, the wedding was just around the corner. Everyone was getting excited now! I just kept hoping I wouldn't fall going down the aisle, and ruin everything. Before I knew it the big day was here and everyone was busy getting ready. We drove to the church. Bonnie was beautiful, and my brother was one of the most handsome men I had ever seen. The church was lovely, and everything looked picture perfect. We each waited for our cue to go down the aisle, and suddenly the music started playing, so I grabbed hold of my brother-in-law's arm and hung on tight, so that I would not only walk straight, but keep my balance. The whole time I was going down the aisle, I couldn't help but wish it were my wedding. When we reached the front of the church, the wedding party turned around while the audience stood up, and the organist began playing the bridal song. I felt so proud of my brother; I could hardly keep from crying. After the wedding, everyone went to the Christopher Columbus Hall for supper. Everyone ate, drank and danced the night away. The music was good, and how I wished Ray was there to dance with! All the excitement was soon over, and it was time for my brother to take his new bride and get out of there. I'm not sure where they went, but I know they were very happy.

After the honeymoon, Bonnie and Ken rented an apartment on Spruce Street. My mother's house seemed really empty without Ken. I was going to have to work on not depending on him so much. I wanted Bonnie to like me. Everything seemed to be going pretty smoothly, so Mom decided she was going to go away for a few days. I would have been okay just staying in my own house, but Ken and Bonnie insisted that I stay with them. They hadn't been married very long at this time, and I felt like I was imposing on them. But, I was glad I had company because my house gave me the creeps at night, when I was there alone. I think the memories of my father being in that house were still fresh. Bonnie would get up in the morning and walk to work. She and Ken had only one car, and he left for work early. When I got up I wanted to be helpful, so I often had lunch ready for her when she came home at noon. After a couple of days, Mom returned from her trip, and I went back home.

The weather was now getting nice outside and the sun felt warm, and the flowers were in bloom. My friend Audrey was working on Mackinac Island, so I didn't get to see her very often. When we did get together we had a lot to talk about. She had met a boyfriend, and that kept her busy. I would go and visit Ray's mother once in a while. For some reason I always felt closer to him when I was at his house. It seemed like I could smell his aftershave lotion. His mom was so nice. She always made me feel welcome.

A TALENT LOST/A LIFE WITH A PURPOSE

There were still no signs that Ray might be able to come home in the near future. Needless to say, this caused me to have many lonely nights. I was glad that I could at least look forward to my job. Working at the hospital was very interesting to me. Every night something different happened. All the girls I worked with were nice. Everyone pitched in and helped each other. About every three or four weeks, a certain woman patient would be admitted to the floor that I usually worked on, and she wouldn't keep her clothes on. That always made the night real interesting. The poor lady didn't know what she was doing. I felt sorry for her. At the end of my shift, I would always check on her to make sure she was okay. After work one particular night, I just rode around in my car listening to the radio. This time of night, the station I listened to played a lot of sad songs that I could relate to. After about an hour of riding around listening to sad songs, and feeling sorry for myself, I went home and went straight to bed.

The Summer of '64

It was now the middle of July 1964. The weather was nice, and I would lie in the sun almost every afternoon before I went to work. I was getting a nice tan—probably the best tan I had in years. Once in a while, Audrey and I would go to Sherman Park, and just lie in the sun, and dream of our futures. My sister and her family—from Marshall, Michigan—would come for weekend visits. My sister's kids were getting pretty big. I enjoyed having them home. The house seemed to come alive again, with the noise of children laughing and playing. Big meals were planned, and many family stories were told.

The summer seemed to be going by faster than I thought it would. My brother, Ken's, wedding to Bonnie Killips in June was one of the highlights of the season. I didn't do much but work and sleep, but I think the excitement of Ken's wedding made the days pass quicker. I looked forward to autumn. I always liked the fall—looking at all the pretty colors on the trees, and listening to the leaves rustle beneath my feet every time I took a step. It was always a special time for my father, as he reveled in the deer hunting ritual at the family camp at Rockford, Michigan. This was now the second fall that Dad was not with us to "bring home the venison" from deer camp.

One beautiful day, Audrey and I decided to go for a ride out past the village of Pickford. The apples were getting ripe on all the apple trees. As we passed some farms, we looked in their fields to see if they had any apple trees. Sure enough, we saw an apple tree full of nice red apples. Audrey and I looked at each other, and we both had the same thought, at the same time. We stopped the car and began picking a few apples. After all, who would miss two or three apples? Well, I guess the farmer who owned the tree did, because he began shooting at us. We didn't know if he had real bullets in his gun, but we weren't sticking around to find out! We left real quickly, just in case he decided to follow us. The farmer didn't follow us, so we continued on our way. This was a day we weren't going to forget for a while! After all that, the apples weren't very good anyway. We drove home, cleaned up and went to a movie. The day ended and we were still alive and very tired. We said goodbye, and went to our own homes for the night—the next day meant work for both of us.

It seemed like everyone was into doing his or her own thing now. Most of my classmates were either in college, or had moved out of town. I was getting very uneasy about my future, and I wasn't really sure what mine would be. Ray had been gone almost a year, and was now stationed in California—he wasn't writing as often as he used to. He said he was very busy every day. I was beginning to doubt whether we were ever going to get married, and I was lonely. I think I didn't write as often as I used to, either. He called me one night when he had too much to drink— I could tell that by the way he was talking. This really made me angry. I thought, he finally calls me, and he is drunk. I tried not to think about him anymore, but he was always on my mind.

Winter '64

Winter was just around the corner, and I knew this would bring all kinds of new challenges for me, especially getting my car started in the cold weather! Just getting around in the snow was hard for me. I still lost my balance easily. The winter started with a bang. We had a big snowstorm, and there was only my mother and me to do the shoveling. When I would get off work at 11:30 at night, it meant digging my way into the driveway every night. Once in a while my neighbors would still be up, and they would come outside and help me shovel. Some days it was snowing too hard, and I was worried my car wouldn't start when I got off work. So I would occasionally take a taxi to and from work.

This seemed to work out pretty well, except for the day I drove to work when the weather was okay. But, while I was working the snow began to blow, and before I knew what was happening, a big storm was brewing. Nobody could leave early, because the hospital was very busy. When my shift was over, I went to my car—and sure enough, it wouldn't start. I tried to get a taxi, but there weren't any taxis available because the storm was too bad, and they couldn't get through the snow. The streets weren't being plowed, and it made it almost impossible for cars to get through the heavy snow. I called my mother, hoping she would try to come and get me. I didn't know what else to do. My mother said there wasn't any way she could come and get me. She suggested I stay at the hospital for the night. I guess I can't blame her for not wanting to come and get me, but there was no way I could stay at the hospital.

A TALENT LOST/A LIFE WITH A PURPOSE

I took a deep breath, and decided to try to walk home. I was doomed from the beginning of my journey! The roads were covered with snow, there weren't any sidewalks, and the snow was coming down thick, covering my footprints as fast as I took a step. I didn't have very good balance to begin with, and now it was almost impossible for me to stay on my feet. However, being the stubborn person that I am, I kept going.

My mother's house is a long way from the hospital, and tonight it seemed even further. Ken and Bonnie's apartment was closer to the hospital than my mother's house. I thought if I could make it that far, I would know that I didn't have much further to go. However, just as I was almost in front of Ken's apartment, I fell and couldn't get up for a few minutes. I knew I couldn't lie in the middle of the street all night. Besides, if I stayed there, I would get pretty cold. I finally made it to my feet but it felt like I might have broken something. I limped into my brother's front porch. Not wanting to wake them up, I cuddled in the corner of the porch and tried to keep warm. I sat there for a long time, and waited until it started to get daylight. I was hoping I would feel better by then, and could leave before anyone in the house woke up and found me sitting there. The snow had quit falling, and everything seemed a lot better in the early morning. I got to my feet and headed for home. My mother didn't even miss me. She thought I had stayed at the hospital all night.

By the time I got up for the day, my mother had left for work. I didn't tell anybody about the exciting night I had in the snowstorm. There was a lot of snow everywhere you looked. This meant shoveling before the taxi could pick me up for work. I had left my car in the parking lot at the hospital the night before. The only thing I could think of was to once again ask my brother to help me get my car started before I had to go on my shift. I called Ken at work, and he said he would help me on his lunch hour. This was great for me, but probably meant not much time for lunch for him.

The car started after a little coaxing from Ken. I remember thinking, "Great, no more walking in the middle of the night for me for a while." I thanked Ken, and hoped he knew how much I appreciated all his help. I knew I was not only imposing on him, but I was also imposing on his new bride. They usually had lunch together, but because of me, they weren't having lunch together that day.

My routine at work was fairly quiet. I carried out the usual bed sheet straightening, and completed my rounds with back rubs just before the lights were turned out for the night. I recall that one of my patients had a lot of hair on his back. I couldn't imagine that any man could be so hairy! This gentleman informed me that this is what gave him sex appeal around women. I laughed about that, because I found all that hair was not attractive to me at all. Another thing, the lotion that the hospital used just made a sticky mess on his back. It wouldn't rub into his skin. When my shift was nearing the end, I wondered if my car was going to start. I was lucky, as it started right up. I would not have wanted to try navigating the cold, snowbound streets again.

Thanksgiving, 1964

Another Thanksgiving holiday was approaching, and my mother informed me that she wouldn't be home on Thanksgiving Day this year. So again, I let everyone know that if they wanted me to work for them, I was available. I preferred to work, rather than being by myself, thinking of Ray. Of course, there were plenty of coworkers who jumped at the chance to spend Thanksgiving with their families. At least I could get a traditional Thanksgiving meal at the hospital cafeteria. Actually, the food was not that bad. For company, there were some nurses who came and sat down with me for our big dinner. We had as much fun as anyone could, in our half-hour break. Afterward, it was time to get our patients ready for bed.

When I finished my shift, I went straight home. The streets didn't have any cars on them this late at night. At first I started to feel real sorry for myself for being alone on this holiday, but I rationalized that things would be better in the future. When I got home, the phone was ringing—it was Ray calling to wish me a happy turkey day. It sure was great hearing from him. I guess he was still thinking of me after all. We talked for quite a while, and then he told me he wouldn't be home for Christmas again this year. But, he thought he might be able to come home in January. I was so disappointed that he wouldn't be home for Christmas, but he sounded like he was sad, too. So, I didn't say much about him not being able to make it. The phone call made my night, and things didn't seem so bad. Just hearing his voice enabled me to go to sleep.

The next day, I kept going over and over our conversation from the night before. Of course, I kept counting the times he told me he loved me. This meant so much to me because it was hard for me to believe anybody could love me. I was just a broken-up person, without any talent. I knew I should quit thinking like this, but I just couldn't figure out how to feel better about myself. It was also getting harder and harder to stay true blue for Ray when he was so far away. I was getting so lonely; it even crossed my mind to go out with someone else. I couldn't imagine whom; I just wanted to be taken out on a date. I figured that if he had the opportunity to see other girls, then perhaps I should date as well. I did date a few times, but Ray was never far from my thoughts. When Christmas rolled around, I decided to work so that someone with a family could have the day off. A couple of days after Christmas, Mom and I went to Aunt Pearl's in Canada. That was always a fun trip to make, and the food was always great, and plentiful.

Everyone at work was now gearing up for the New Year holiday. Ken's friend and his wife were planning a New Year's Eve party, and Ken invited me to come over after I got off work that night. The party was right across the street, so I figured I didn't have far to go. I thought a party would do me some good. Ken and Bonnie loved to dance, and they were fun to watch. At the party, Ken grabbed me and pulled me on to the dance area, and started twirling me around and around. As I was twirling, I lost my balance, and fell right on my butt! I wasn't hurt, but I was really embarrassed. I scraped myself up off the floor, and decided that was it for me, as far as the dancing goes. I was just glad to be out with people, laughing and joking. After the party broke up, I went home to crawl in bed and think about the new year ahead.

Now that January had come, I looked forward to Ray coming home. He called me one night to tell me that he wasn't sure of the dates, but he was putting together the plans to come home in about two or three weeks. I was so excited, I couldn't stand it! Then, a guy I had known from high school called to ask me out on a Saturday night. I accepted, as I thought it would be fun. But, I got a big surprise on the day that I was supposed to go out with that other guy—Ray called and said he was in town, and was coming right over. I quickly called my date, and told him I couldn't go out that night. Whew, that was close! Now I was ready to see Ray, who had been gone for over a year. I wondered if he would be the same, and if I would still feel the same toward to him. When I saw his car turn in the driveway, I knew that the spark was still there, and that my feelings for him were as strong as ever.

Ray reacted just perfectly toward me. I knew that in his big strong arms was right where I wanted to be, feeling secure and safe. I also knew that he was not leaving without me for another year of separation. I talked to him about my feelings, but he was afraid of a commitment. As the days went by, I would ask him if marriage was in the cards. Nothing was getting settled, so one day I encouraged him to make up his mind. I knew that if a wedding were going to take place, plans would have to be made quickly. Then he just came right out with it, and asked me to be his bride. I didn't have to hesitate for one minute to give him my answer. Of course, the answer was YES! I was so excited that I could have yelled: "Listen, everybody, I'm getting married to the man I love!"

The Night Ray Asked Me to Marry Him

The night he asked me to marry him was a Saturday. We decided to get married the following Saturday night. There sure was a lot to do in one week. But I made up my mind it could be done. The first order of business was to tell our parents. I was sure they would be shocked, but I didn't think they would give us a hard time. We decided we had better tell them right away, mainly because they only had about an hour to get used to the idea. There simply wasn't much time to sit and discuss the issue.

First we went to Ray's parents. They weren't thrilled with the idea, but didn't say anything. Now it was time to tell my mother. I knew it could go either way with her. She could be happy for us or be a real stinker. Well, she decided to be very negative about the whole idea of getting married so soon. First, she asked if we were sure that this is what we wanted to do? Then she proceeded to ask Ray to show her how he thought he could support me. Poor Ray got a piece of paper and tried to show her how we could make it work. But she couldn't or didn't want to see how we thought we could manage. After she put Ray through his paces for a couple of hours, I just told her we were getting married with or without her blessing. The next day I scheduled our blood work, booked the church, talked to the minister, ordered flowers and looked for a wedding dress. Oh, I also had to go to work and announce that I would be leaving at the end of the week.

Nothing went very smoothly. My mother wouldn't leave me alone about getting married and even asked Ray if he would please think it over. The minister wouldn't marry us without us taking some counseling classes. I had to make special arrangements to get our blood work done in time. Then, of course, you couldn't have a wedding without a maid of honor and a best man. We knew they should be asked as soon as possible, so we called the people we chose and they were excited for us. It sure was good having someone on our side. Now we had to figure out what they were going to wear. Audrey was my maid of honor, and was about the same size as me. So I asked her if she minded wearing the dress I wore in Ken's wedding. She thought that was a great idea. We also had to get ushers and send out invitations. Oh, I almost forgot, we had to order the wedding cake too. Boy, was I ever busy! I loved every minute of it. Ray bought my dress, bought both of the rings we needed, and was there to hold my hand when I needed to be calmed down.

Next we had to figure out how were we going to get all the way to San Diego. Ray's brother had a car that he had been trying to sell, so Ray bought the car. It was a four-door Ford Falcon, with shiny chrome on the sides. It looked like everything was falling into place. I found a beautiful dress on sale at The Hub, and it fit me perfectly. There was going to be a funeral the morning of our wedding and the minister told us we could use the flowers from the funeral for the altar. This was nice of our minister—I think he knew that we were "pinching pennies"! My brother was happy for me, and said he would be glad to walk me down the aisle.

The girls at work gave me a surprise shower. I was really surprised because I only knew the girls I worked with. There were a lot of people there that I hardly knew. I got some very nice things that would surely come in handy. Audrey and her mother also gave me a shower. I was so excited about how happy everyone seemed for me. It was so nice of everyone. I knew I didn't give anyone much time to prepare, let alone give me a shower. I was a very lucky person to know so many caring people. I just hoped I could return the favors.

LINDA (DALE) COOK

We were planning a lunch in the basement of the church after the wedding, and my mother was busy making cookies for the reception. I appreciated everything my mother was doing, but she was so unhappy that I was getting married that I didn't want to be around her. She fought the wedding right to the end. Our wedding day came and I was so happy I could never put into words how wonderful I felt. The weather was storming outside, but that didn't even bother me. In a few hours I would be Mrs. Raymond Cook, something I had dreamed about for several years. I had begun to think I was never getting married, and now the day was here, and soon I would be with the man I dearly loved for the rest of my life. I thanked the Lord for making my dream come true, and realized He was still watching over me.

It was now time to go to the church and get ready for my wedding. Bonnie and my cousin helped me get my dress on and fixed my headpiece on my head. I had borrowed the headpiece from Bonnie and had my hair done that morning to go with the headpiece. I'm so glad I had help getting ready, because I was really nervous. The music started and the maid of honor and best man began walking down the aisle. I said a little prayer, and suddenly my brother was taking my arm and the music for the wedding march began playing. As I walked down the aisle, all I could see was Ray standing there waiting for me. He looked so handsome I could hardly believe he would soon be my husband. I had a hard time concentrating on what the minister was saying, because I felt any minute I would wake up and all this would be a dream. Then I heard the minister say, "Do you, Linda Dale, take this man to be your husband?" All I could think of was, boy, do I ever! Thank goodness I didn't say that. Instead, I replied with the words "I do!" Then we were pronounced husband and wife. I think I floated back down the aisle with Ray by my side. We went to the lower level of the church and had a very nice lunch. After everyone ate, we opened our gifts. This was so exciting for me.

We got a lot of nice things, and some money too. Then we got into the car as a married couple for the first time. We road around and just honked our horn to let everyone know how happy we were. After riding around for a while, it was now time to go and get ready to leave for California. I had packed my clothes before the wedding, so all I really had to do was change into something to wear for my first trip as the new Mrs. Ray Cook.

It was cold and snowing outside. We loaded as many presents as we could in the car, and we were now on our way. It was getting dark, and both of us were very tired. We only made it as far as St. Ignace, just an hour down the highway. Ray almost fell asleep while he was driving, so we thought we had better stop for the night. When I opened up my suitcase in the motel room, I discovered that my clothes had all been tied together, and they were covered with confetti! Someone had played a trick on me, and I had a good idea who the culprit(s) might be. Ray and I just started laughing. The next morning, it seemed weird waking up with Ray by my side. But, I was secure and content.

After a good breakfast, we headed out for Marshall, Michigan. The plan was to spend the night, and visit with Joyce and Gerald, as they couldn't attend the wedding. The highway we had to travel on our way to California went right by their town. My sister was glad to see us, of course, and I was proud to walk into her house as Mrs. Ray Cook. After supper, we sat around and visited. It was getting late, and we knew that the next day, we would have a long drive ahead of us. We had figured that it would take about four days to reach San Diego. Ray was still on military leave, and we had a couple of extra days built into our plans, before he had to report back for duty. After breakfast the next day, we headed out again. There was a heavy snowfall the night before, but that wouldn't stop us. At least we knew that there wouldn't be any snow in San Diego. As we were heading south, the weather kept getting worse. A huge storm was brewing. It was hard to see very far in front of the 1962 Ford Falcon we were driving. With Ray by my side, I wasn't worried at all. Suddenly, as we were going up a hill on a two-lane highway, we saw a car parked in our driving lane! Our first thought was that the car must be moving very slowly because of the storm, but then we realized that it wasn't moving at all.

The highway was covered with a thick layer of snow and ice. We couldn't go to the right of the stationary car because of the high snow banks. We slowed down, but couldn't completely stop because of the icy conditions. So, Ray's choices were to either hit the car, or go into the oncoming lane and hope that a car wasn't coming up the other side of the hill. Ray decided to take a chance, and go into the oncoming lane. Suddenly we saw a car barreling toward us. Little did we think that a car would be traveling that fast in a snow storm. The approaching car was right in front of us before we knew what was happening. Ray did the only thing he could to try to save us—he headed for the left ditch. In reality, it was a snow-covered ravine. The driver that was coming straight at us also didn't want a head-on collision, so he headed for the same ravine. As our cars smashed, you could hear the metal of each of the cars scraping together. His car went right down the side of our four-door Falcon, from the front to the rear.

Our car was hit hard enough that we were pushed into the ravine quite a distance. Before Ray could even get out of the car, there were four other cars involved in the accident. They hadn't seen the driver in the middle of the road either. Ray looked at me and made sure I was okay, then he got out of the car and headed up the bank to the road. The snow was deep, and both of us were dressed for warmer weather. After all, we were headed for sunny California, and hadn't planned to be forced out into the elements. When Ray reached the side of the road, the man who had caused the accident was standing facing the far snow bank relieving his bladder! We often wondered if he had been drinking, but as far as we know, no one ever received a traffic ticket.

Soon the police and ambulance arrived. Three or four people from the other cars were hurt, and had to be taken to the hospital. I was still sitting in the car where Ray told me to stay. But, I could feel the car settling further in the snow, and there was no way I was staying in that car any longer! I had only a light pair of shoes on, but getting snowy was a lot better than staying in a car that was sinking further into the snow. When I got to the top of the snow bank, the police were questioning the driver that hit us. He was a young guy in his teens. He didn't have a driver's license, or any insurance on the car he was driving. We couldn't figure out why the police didn't give him, or the man that caused all the accidents, a ticket. The wrecker came and pulled our car out of the ravine, and when Ray got in it, the car started right up.

Knowing that we couldn't just continue on to California with the car the way it was, we headed back to Joyce and Gerald's. When we arrived, they were very surprised to see us. They couldn't believe that the car was even still running. We all sat around and tried to decide what to do next. We didn't have much money, or time, so our options were limited. Ray called his commanding officer in San Diego, and got an extension on his leave of absence. Gerald thought that he could straighten out some of the metal, and drill holes to attach a steel plate that would keep the two doors on the right side bolted shut. The car sure looked a mess, but we were just glad that we weren't hurt, and the car was still running. The car wouldn't be ready to travel until the next day, so we spent another night in Marshall. The snow had finally stopped when we headed out once again. Some of our wedding presents were broken in the car accident, but we still had a few things left.

We drove about 400 miles on that first day, then stopped for the night. The next morning we got up and hoped that the car would still run. Oil was leaking from somewhere, so we added more oil in what was once our beautiful teal-colored car.

Whenever we would stop along the way, people would stare at our moving "wreck." When we drove through the desert, the car started to heat up, and we had to stop to let the engine cool off. One time when we pulled over into a small parking area, we saw signs warning us to watch for snakes and poisonous spiders. I sure hadn't seen signs like this back in Michigan! I had no desire to linger any longer than we needed to. We got back in the car and continued our journey west. After yet another overnight rest, we headed out, only to be nearly run down by a semi-truck driver who ran a red light. This gave us a real scare, so we pulled over and went into a restaurant and had a soda pop to calm our nerves. It was a good thing that we were newly married, and crazy about being together—a lot of what happened the last few days could have bothered us a lot more.

Ray would rarely let me drive, but one night we were still on the road as it was getting dark. Ray was really tired, and we knew we had to drive further, or we wouldn't make California before his leave was over. We had little choice, but for me to drive. We were just heading into the mountains, and the scenery was beautiful. It was now quite dark, and everyone had their headlights on. Ray had just fallen asleep, and I didn't want to wake him up. Every time that I would pass an oncoming vehicle, people would honk their horn. I couldn't figure out what was wrong, so I finally woke Ray and told him what was going on. Ray opened his eyes and realized that I had been driving too far to the left as the roadway curved around the mountains, and the oncoming traffic was being forced to the edge of the cliff! Ray took over the driving after that, and there was no more honking from the other lane. Then we started coming out of the mountains into Albuquerque, New Mexico. The city was all lit up in the dark night, like a string of multi-colored pearls. It was almost breathtaking—I had never seen anything so beautiful.

The further west we went, the warmer it became. It was hard to believe that just a few days before, we were in a snowstorm! It was the first time that I had ever gone from full-blown winter weather to summer weather. I thought that this was great. We drove, and drove, only to stop late at night to sleep. Just as we were getting near Pasadena, California, Ray said, "I have cousins that live in this town. Would you like to stop and see them?" I thought that it might be nice meeting a relative Ray hadn't seen for a long time. So, we found the house, and went to the door and knocked. We didn't think anyone was home, when finally his cousin appeared at the door. It was the first time I visited a member of Ray's family as Mrs. Ray Cook. It felt good when he introduced me as his wife. We visited for a while, and then we were on our way again for San Diego. I can't remember just how long it took for this final leg of our long drive across the country, but I know that I was filled with excitement, knowing that we were reaching our final destination.

When we finally arrived, the sun had already set. I can't describe the feeling I had when we entered the city that was to be my home for the next two years! It was unbelievable—we had made the long journey, and we were still "in one piece." It was getting late, and we knew that we had to find a place to stay for the night. We thought that we had better count what little money we had left. The trip had cost us more than what we had expected. The reasons were obvious, of course. The car accident and the money we spent on oil had set us back a little. One solution to our money problem was to get a refund for Ray's airline ticket, as he had planned to fly back instead of driving. It was too late to do this that night, so we used most of our last 40 dollars to get a motel room for the night. The next day, we had just enough money for breakfast, then we went to the airport to return his unused ticket. We now had about two dollars left from the 40, and 95 from his returned ticket. We knew that we didn't have much money to find an apartment, but we were in love, and our meager finances didn't seem to matter very much.

I just took it for granted that it would be easy to find some place to live. Well, we began looking. It seemed like we looked at a lot of places, and they were either too small, or out of our price range. We were both getting tired by the end of our first day of searching. Ray turned down a street, and we saw a real cute apartment complex, with a grassy courtyard in the middle. There was a vacancy sign in the yard, but we thought that the apartments looked too nice for the amount of money we had. We decided to find out anyway. The owner seemed very nice, and Ray explained that we were a Navy couple and didn't have much money, but payday was at the end of the week. To our surprise, the owner said he would take a down payment, and we could pay him the rest of the rent on Friday. The apartment was nice, completely repainted, and the furnishings seemed new. I couldn't believe it, it looked perfect—just what we were looking for. We hauled everything out of the car for the first time since our wedding. We put just enough things away so that we could get to bed. Ray had to leave early the next morning to go back to the Navy base on North Island. I was too tired to even think about being alone in such a big city. The next morning came quickly, and Ray had to leave me for four days, as he had weekend "duty watch." He had me drive him down to the ferry, at the foot of Market Street, in San Diego. I really began to worry, as I would have to drive back to the apartment, and I had never driven on streets like this, where there were more than two lanes!

Getting Lost in San Diego

    I went back to the apartment to sit quietly by myself, and get calmed down before it was time to go and get Ray. I could hardly wait to see him, but yet I was scared silly of having to drive down to the place where I was supposed to pick him up. It would be getting dark at the time I was to leave to go get him. I was afraid I wouldn't recognize any of the places he told me to look for on the way, to let me know I was going in the right direction. The rest of the day went pretty fast, because I had something to look forward to. My man was coming home, and he would have some money to buy some food (which I thought would be great, because by now, I was pretty hungry). The big moment finally came! I went and got in my smashed-up car that looked like a piece of junk. The car started right up, and still had lots of gas in it. I was so nervous that I was shaking. I kept telling myself, you can do it, just calm down.

    I drove to the first corner where I had to decide, do I turn left or right? I thought I would know which way to turn. But when I got to the corner, I wasn't sure which direction to go. Everything looked so different after dark. I took a guess, and nothing looked familiar, but I thought if I kept driving I would recognize something. When I drove over an overpass and started heading onto a highway that had eight lanes, I knew something was wrong. Ray and I didn't drive on an overpass, or on an eight-lane freeway! Now I was really scared! I looked for the first exit and took it. Now I figured I was lost for sure. At least I wasn't on the highway anymore. I was now driving on regular streets. I drove for a little while, and I was getting more confused by the minute.

I saw a little grocery store, and I thought I would go in and ask for some directions. As I went to get out of the car, a little boy approached the car and kept saying over and over; "Are you lost, lady?" After all my experiences the last few days, it would be best if I didn't speak to the little boy. I went into the store, and all the people working in the store were either Mexicans or black people. The Mexicans didn't speak English, and the blacks wouldn't talk to me. I left the store and got back into my car.

    I wasn't sure what to do next, but I knew I couldn't stay where I was. I figured I wasn't in an area where white people were welcomed with open arms. I began to drive around some more, just getting more lost all the time. I saw another store and I decided to go in and see if they would give me some directions. The only place I could park my car was on a little incline, and directly behind my car about a half block away was a very busy intersection. I got out of my car and went into the store and the store personnel were an unfamiliar nationality, but seemed very friendly. However, they didn't speak very good English and they repeated different street names. But, I didn't know the name of the street I lived on, let alone any other street names! As I left the store, I looked for my car—it had rolled down the hill into the busy intersection! I was so upset by now, I decided I would get into my car, and probably be killed from another car hitting me. My other choice wasn't any better, because I figured if I didn't get into my car soon, I would probably be mugged! I opened the door of my car, got into it, and put my head down waiting to be hit. After a few minutes of waiting for another car to hit me, and nothing was happening, I raised my head and couldn't believe my eyes. All the traffic had stopped. I thought maybe I was dreaming, but suddenly I realized I was still alive. So I started my car and got out of there as fast as I could. I drove about a block when I saw a gas station. I pulled my car into the station, got out of the car and went in to tell the attendant that I was lost, and I wasn't getting back into my car.

To my surprise, the man I was talking to was the owner of my apartment! He recognized me, and said he would be glad to help me. I'm sure he saw how upset I was, so he told me he would give me directions. I said thank you, but I quickly added, "But, sir, I'm not driving the car any more tonight." Then, he asked exactly where it was that I was supposed to pick up Ray. I tried to explain to him, but at this point I don't think I was making too much sense. He said, "Never mind, I'll find it—get in the car, and I will drive you to your husband." I knew I was taking a chance getting in the car with a stranger. But, I didn't think I had much of a choice. He took me right where I needed to go. Ray was standing there waiting for me. When Ray opened the car door, he immediately saw this man, and wondered what on earth I was doing with this guy. Then he recognized the man as the owner of our apartment. Ray asked what took me so long, as he had been waiting for a long time. When I started to tell him what happened, he just laughed. I guess he didn't realize how upset I had been. He got in the car, and we drove the man back there. When we got to the gas station, Ray pointed out to me that the whole time I was lost, I was never more than four or five blocks from where we lived. In fact, the gas station where the owner of our apartment was, is just a street away from where we lived. Boy, did I feel stupid when I realized that all this time I was so scared because I thought I was lost, when I was only blocks away from home.

When we left the gas station, we went straight to the grocery store, and bought ingredients to make spaghetti and meatballs. After we ate supper, Ray decided we should practice driving the route to the ferry dock a couple of times. He wanted to make sure I didn't have any trouble picking him up the following night. I watched very closely, noting every turn Ray made, and everything he showed me that was near our street. I didn't want to think any more this evening, about what had happened. I just wanted to enjoy having Ray with me.

LINDA (DALE) COOK

We still didn't have a TV or anything for entertaining ourselves, but we didn't care because we had each other. It was now time to go to bed, and things didn't seem scary with Ray at home. The funny thing was that when Ray was home, nothing crazy ever happened! The morning came too soon, because Ray had to be back on base by eight o'clock. On our way to the ferry, I started to get sad again. It seemed like I had only seen him for a few hours since we arrived in San Diego. We got to the ferry, and parked the car where we were supposed to, and Ray got out and kissed me goodbye. I sat and watched him until he disappeared out of sight. Now I knew it was time to see if I could remember everything Ray had told me the night before, about how to get back home. As I drove up Market Street, I was shaking like a leaf. But, this time, I recognized several things that I had been watching for. Before I knew it, there in plain sight was the corner I had to turn on, to go up my street. When I arrived in front of our apartment, I tried to park the car closer to the top of the hill, so the car wouldn't be on such a slant, and leak gas onto the street. I got out of the car, and went inside our apartment.

I began to plan a few things I could do. Ray had brought home some dirty clothes that I could wash, and I could make a cherry pie for his supper tonight. Everything seemed so much better today, just knowing Ray was coming home at suppertime. Ray had shown me were there was a Laundromat just down the alley from where we lived. I made the bed, picked up the apartment, did the laundry and baked a cherry pie. I enjoyed every minute of doing these things. After all, it was the first time I had ever done his laundry, or baked him his favorite pie. When I had completed everything I could think of to keep busy, I took a nap. I figured that when I woke up, it would be almost time to go and pick Ray up at what the Navy guys called the "nickel snatcher" (the ferry boat).

I took a nap for a couple of hours, woke up, and couldn't wait to go get Ray. I drove straight to the ferry. He was standing there looking so handsome in his sailor uniform. I waved to him, and he came and got into the car right away. We really seemed like we were a married couple now. We decided to go through the drive-through at the Jack In the Box, and then go home for dessert. Ray enjoyed the cherry pie I made him.

    This evening we went sightseeing. There was so much to see. Ray drove me down and showed me what Broadway looked like. I had never seen any place like Broadway. It is difficult to explain the awe I felt. I guess the best way to describe it is that it is very glamorous, and yet kind of sad, too. There were tattoo parlors and shops that lured enlisted men in, tempting them to buy a bunch of things they probably didn't need. On the sad side, there were real bag ladies, and lots of homeless people. After showing me Broadway, Ray took me down by the water, and we walked down on the dock to look at some Navy ships that were tied up to shore. The fresh air felt so good. The weather in San Diego was perfect. Everything was beautiful. There were beautiful flowers everywhere, and I had never seen a palm tree. Everyone's yard looked like it had been manicured.

Finding a New Apartment

This evening was what I had pictured in my mind—Ray and me in San Diego. There was so much to see, and all the things I had seen in a book, or on TV, were right at my fingertips. I kept thinking how lucky I was. Everything that had gone wrong seemed so far away right now. There were just Ray and me with the bright moon shining over the entire city. As I felt Ray's big strong arms circle my body, I felt so safe and secure. What a beautiful night! I didn't have to share Ray with anyone, and the only thing that shined brighter than his eyes was the beautiful moon above. The moon was so bright it put a romantic glow on everything. Yes, this certainly was a night for two people that were in love. I didn't want this evening to end, but unfortunately it was getting late, and Ray had to get up early so he could be back on base on time. We went home and listened to the radio for a while, and then went to bed.

Once again, it was morning, and I was faced with the trip down to the ferry. It was getting easier for me to find my way back home after dropping Ray off. I still got nervous, but managed to get back to our apartment. Once I got to our apartment, though, I never went anywhere except down the alley to do the laundry. Ray was coming home tonight, and then had two whole days off. The day dragged by, because there wasn't anything for me to do but take a nap. I kept watching the time, anxious for four o'clock to come, so I could go and pick up my man from work. I drove down to the ferry, and he was standing there just as I had pictured him all day. Yes, indeed, I loved a uniform on a man, especially this man! He was sure easy on the eyes. Ray had a tailored uniform that fit his little body like a glove. I was so proud to be his wife, I felt sure every woman envied me. As he got into the car, a warm feeling always went through my body.

This time as we went home, I knew he didn't have to go back to the base for two whole days! We went sightseeing every day. There always seemed to be a lot of things we hadn't seen before. We were on a very limited income, so it didn't even cross our mind to do anything that would cost money. It didn't matter to me as long as we were together. Even though we were having a good time, I kept thinking that after these two days, Ray is going to be gone again for another four days. For supper we went to a Taco Bell. I had never seen a fast-food restaurant like this. It was one of the first times I had ever eaten a taco. The taco was pretty good. After we ate, we went to a mall just to look around. Their malls sometimes even had cars and huge fountains in them. I thought, if the people at home in the Soo could only see what malls could look like, they sure would be surprised. After looking around for a while, we decided we had better head for home. We talked for a bit and listened to the radio, and then went to sleep.

When I dropped Ray off the next time, I knew I wouldn't hear or see from him for four days. This always made me very depressed. I still didn't know anyone and we didn't have a TV yet. The first night went okay; the second night somebody kept playing with the fuse box that was outside of our apartment and my lights would go off and on. I just stayed real still and after a while they would quit. I made it through another night, but was really lonesome and wished I had somebody to talk to. I didn't have many clothes to wash, but I thought going to the Laundromat would give me something to do, and I would be with some other people even if I didn't know them. When I went to the Laundromat, the owner of our apartment was there with his wife. She started talking to me and I was glad to get to know her.

The building owner's wife seemed really nice, and I think she saw how lonely I was. She asked me over to her house for supper, saying they were going to grill hamburgers. I accepted the invitation right away. I was so happy to have someone to talk to, and eat with. Her house was just around the corner from where we lived. So, I knew I wouldn't have any problem finding her house. I drove over to her house because I thought it might be dark when I came back home and I discovered we were living in a pretty bad neighborhood. I had a nice time at her house and she made me feel welcome. When it was time to go home, her husband said maybe it would be a good idea to follow me home to make sure I got into my apartment okay. I thought it was really nice of this guy to care whether I got home safely or not. So I told him following me home would be great, because, if the truth was known, I was scared to go by myself anyway. He followed behind my car and as I parked, he pulled his car in behind mine, and got out. He said he would walk me to the door and see that I got my lights on.

I was thinking, what a gentleman! But when we stepped into the apartment and I reached for the light switch, he shut the door behind him. I wondered what he was doing, when all of a sudden he grabbed me and started to kiss me. I was shocked, because he had seemed like such nice man. I pushed him away and blurted out, "If you don't leave, I'm going to tell your wife." He let me go and said, "Isn't this what you wanted?" I told him, "You have to be kidding." With this, he left my apartment, but I worried all night that he would come back, and I wondered if he had a master key to get in. I decide right then that this was the end of living here, if I could convince Ray to move. The next day I saw our landlord in the courtyard. I stayed in my apartment and kept the blinds pulled. The day couldn't go fast enough, as far as I was concerned. He made me feel really creepy. I could hardly wait to tell Ray about this terrible man.

I went to pick up Ray at the usual time and place. He was standing waiting for me—I was so glad to see him. When he got in the car I didn't say anything right away about our landlord. I let Ray tell me about his day first. Then he asked me how everything went for me while he was gone? I began to tell him all about my experience, thinking he would really be upset with our landlord. But he didn't even get upset, or seem to worry about me staying in the apartment by myself. When I asked him about moving, he just said we couldn't afford any other place right now. I didn't say anything else to him about moving. But I had made up my mind I wasn't going to ever stay in this apartment by myself again.

The next day after I dropped Ray off at the ferry, I decided to go apartment hunting. This was a very big adventure for me because I hadn't driven the car anywhere but to the ferry, since the night I got lost—other than to the owner's house to have a barbecue. I thought I would begin looking close to where we were living, but I didn't see anything I was interested in. Besides, I think the further away from our apartment we moved, the better I would feel. So, I got real brave, and drove several miles from where we were living. I saw a very beautiful apartment complex called Capri Terrace, on the residential part of Broadway Street. This place looked perfect to me, only it looked way out of our price range. I decided to go and look at the apartment anyway. After all, it wouldn't hurt to look. I went to the office and told the manager what I was looking for, and she said she had a one-bedroom apartment available. Would I like to see it? I said yes, even though I was thinking we would never be able to afford this place.

The apartment she showed me was exactly what I wanted. There was a front and a back door that led to a completely furnished patio. There also was a Laundromat in the center of the complex, just for the tenants to use. I was scared to ask how much the rent was. But, after she showed me everything, she told me how much the rent would be. I knew we couldn't afford it, but I found myself saying, "Okay, we will take it." I told her that my husband was in the Navy, and he was on North Island right now, but when he came home, I would bring him by to see the apartment. The lady was so nice, she said that would be fine, just stop by and get her, and she would unlock the door for us. I was so excited, he couldn't say no when he saw how happy I was, could he? I went and picked him up, and as soon as he got in the car I blurted out my big news about finding an apartment. He didn't seem overly excited, but he said he would look at the apartment. He was impressed when he saw the outside of the building. Everything looked picture perfect with manicured grounds, and painted stucco exterior. I said to him, if you like this, wait until you see the apartment. We met the landlord and right away Ray thought she was pleasant and friendly.

When Ray saw the inside of the apartment and saw the patio at our back door and the Laundromat in the center of the complex, he was sold on moving. He just wasn't sure how we could afford such a nice place. Right away, I told him I would start looking for work to help pay the rent. He looked at me and could see how much I wanted it. He said all right, we would manage somehow. We gave our new landlord a rent deposit and the apartment was now officially ours. I could hardly wait to move in. The next thing we had to do is tell our old landlord we were moving. We hadn't signed a lease, so I didn't think there would be a problem.

It wouldn't take much to move us because everything we owned would fit in the car. Ray thought it might be better to wait until the next day to tell our old landlord that we found some place else to live. It was getting late, and we weren't sure where to find him. I think Ray was excited about our new apartment, too. The next day Ray went to the base, and when he came home, we told our landlord that we found a bigger apartment and we would be moving right away. He never said much, except we couldn't get our deposit back. But we didn't care; I just wanted to get out of there. We started to move all of our belongings over to the new apartment that very night. We were completely moved by nine o'clock. We were ready to spend the very first night in our new apartment! I knew Ray would be gone for four days starting the next day, but I didn't mind as much as I did before. This apartment was so bright and cheerful, and I was already planning on what I could do to make it more like a home. We were told that there were quite a few other Navy families in this apartment building. I was anxious to meet some of the other wives.

Working at Ratner's of California

Ray had a friend named Jimmy Upton who also was in the Navy. When I came to San Diego, Jimmy and his wife, Kay, who was from San Diego, decided it would be fun for the four of us to get together. When Ray came home and told me we had been invited over to their house for supper and to play cards after we ate, I was so happy. I was hoping we could become friends and we did. We hit it off right away. Kay was very nice and liked to laugh a lot. She helped me get an interview at the factory where she worked. I knew I had to get a job so we could afford the new apartment I had found. She took me to my interview at Ratner's of California, a clothing factory that made men's suit jackets. I got the job, but I was nervous since I had never worked in a factory before. I was hired to inspect finished jackets. I was in for a big surprise, because I never had any idea how difficult factory work would be. I was glad that Kay offered to pick me up to take me to work on my first day.

I was nervous, but Kay was so friendly, and liked to talk. I felt a little more relaxed after talking with her. The ride to the factory led us straight down Market Street, through the heart of San Diego. This area was one the rougher districts of San Diego. Riding down Market Street was sure an eye-opener for me. I saw all kinds of strange people, from drunks to people that lived on the street. We finally arrived at the factory, and it was a huge building—about four or five stories high. I began to wonder what floor I would be working on. There was a truck with a side that opened up that sold all kinds of things to eat. There was a large crowd of people standing in line waiting to be served. Kay explained to me that people bought their breakfast off of the truck each morning. The truck didn't sell things like eggs, but it had a variety of rolls, coffee and juices. Little did I know that soon I would be one of those waiting in line each morning.

Kay knew a lot of people, and everyone seemed friendly toward her. You could tell that Kay had worked there for several years, because she knew right where I had to go. We walked up three flights of stairs and into a big room full of tables, sewing machines, big presses and racks and racks of suit jackets. I had never been in a factory before, and this isn't how I imagined it would look. I don't know what I expected, but I do know this isn't what I thought it would be like. Off to one side was a little office, and a small blonde lady was there and pleasantly smiled and said hello, and introduced herself and asked if I was Linda? Kay said goodbye, and said she would come and get me for lunch. The woman began asking me questions, and explained what my job would be. The title of my job was coat inspector.

After inspecting a coat, I was the person to put a number in the pocket that would show that the item was inspected by No. 11. This didn't seem too difficult to do. I was sure I could handle this "no brainer" job. My new boss walked me to the table where I was to work. Everyone at the table spoke to me but kept working—they seemed to be working as fast as they could. Soon I found out why everyone seemed to be in a hurry. The kind of work I would be doing was called "piecework." This meant you were paid by the number of jackets you inspected, and you had to inspect a certain number of jackets each day or you were fired. The morning went fast because of all the new things I was trying to learn. Then it was lunchtime. A horn blew and everyone began to walk almost in a run. Just imagine three hundred people running around, all going different directions at once!

The scene unfolding before me was very chaotic, and I feared that if I got in anyone's way, I would be trampled on. I just stood safely by my table and wasn't quite sure what to do. Finally I saw Kay. She grabbed my arm and told me to follow her. She started at a slow run, and I had a hard time keeping up with her. We went to some stairs and climbed two more flights up. This meant I was now on the fifth floor. We walked over to her table and jumped up and sat on top of the table and ate the lunch each of us had brought from home. I no sooner started eating the second part of my sandwich when another horn blew, and everyone started running in different directions again. It didn't take me long to figure out this was the end of lunchtime. I hopped down off the table and began a slow run myself, down the stairs to where my table was. I then remembered I had to go to the bathroom, but another horn had blown, and this meant everyone had better be working again. I guess I just had to miss going to the bathroom, and remember to move faster tomorrow, so that I would have time to take a potty break. I also thought a big factory like this would have a cafeteria on one of the floors. But there didn't even seem to be a break room. I figured that I would just have to get used to the way things were.

 Behind where I stood was a big press that was always being used, and steam would roll out every time they pressed anything. I not only inspected each jacket, but I had to take a marker and color each buttonhole black. I couldn't figure out why they didn't use black thread in the first place. I did my job and didn't ask questions. I soon found out that this wasn't as easy as I thought it would be. It was very difficult making the quota at the end of the day. When you needed more jackets to inspect, you had to walk almost to the other side of the building to get them. Then you could only take as many as you could carry. The route back involved going in and out between the tables, carrying an armload of jackets. Once you got them back to your table, you had to hang them up and start the process of checking them. Next, you started looking at the jackets real close. I might find four or five jackets without linings, or perhaps one was missing a sleeve. The jackets that weren't complete would then have to be carried back to where you got them. This seemed like a lot of running around to me—I was sure there must be some shortcut I could take. I started watching my coworkers, and that was exactly the way they did their work. Now I was beginning to wonder if I would ever be able to make the quota for each day. The horn blew and I figured it was time to quit. I was glad the day was over because my back felt like it was broken. It hurt so bad I felt like crying. When Kay came to get me to show me the way out of there, I told her about my back, and she just said it would get better. I sure did hope so.

On our ride down to the ferry to pick up our husbands, Kay assured me it would get easier after I had been there for a while. I was exhausted, but I was glad to see Ray. I could hardly wait to tell him about everything I had done. When I got home my back hurt so bad I just wanted to lie down. But Ray, being a typical man, said, "After you make supper, why don't you lay down for a while, hon." I finished making supper, and fumed the whole time, but didn't say a word about my back. As soon as supper was over, I did go and lie down. After lying there for a while, my back began to feel a lot better. So I got up and watched TV, on a little black-and-white TV that Ray had bought from a friend of his.

It was the morning of day two on the job. After we got our juice and roll, Kay and I headed into the factory. We just had time to get to our tables, eat our roll, and drink our juice before the horn blew. As we passed some Spanish speaking women, they smiled and said something in Spanish. I wasn't sure what they said, but they smiled—so it couldn't have been anything terrible. I had the same routine as the first day, and it didn't seem any easier. In fact, I think my back hurt more than ever. Luckily, the girls at my table were very helpful. When there was something I wasn't sure of, they were more than willing to assist me. Everyone did seem to speak English. In fact, the husband of one of the girls at my table was also in the Navy. We became friends right away. I was having trouble making my quota. I knew somehow that I was going to have to learn to make some shortcuts somewhere. I just hadn't figured out where yet. The horn blew—it was time to leave. The big race began—to get to the stairs, down, and out the door. It still seemed strange to me to see so many people running around like crazy, trying to be the first one out of the door.

Kay had a meeting or something to go to that day, so I was on my own. At the end of the day, I went straight to where I parked my car, and hoped I knew the route to take to go pick up Ray. Driving from the factory to get Ray turned out to be easy, because I didn't have to make any turns. When I got to the ferry, I didn't see Ray, and I began to wonder if there were two places that looked alike—and somehow I was at the wrong place! Just as I was starting to get all worried, I saw Ray walking down the street. The ferry was delayed, so he was a little late. He got in the car and we went home, I got cleaned up, and we went to Taco Bell for supper.

One day led into the other, and pretty soon a month had gone by. I was finally beginning to understand the routine at the factory. I was even making my quota now! One new thing I learned was that every Friday most of the girls went out for lunch. It didn't seem very practical to me, because of where the restaurant was located. It was two blocks away, and we only had half an hour for lunch. This meant going down three flights of stairs that were packed with people, and then running for two blocks to eat. You would have to eat as fast as you could, run two blocks back to the factory, and climb three flights of stairs to get to your table before the horn blew! To begin with, everyone was on their feet for three or four hours without a break. What I wanted to do, more than anything, was to sit down—even if it had to be on top of the table I was working at! It certainly wasn't spending my whole lunch hour running around. I guess I shouldn't complain, because nobody made me go to the restaurant. I was just trying so hard to fit in with the group. I thought it would be better if I followed what they did.

Physically, I just wasn't feeling right and I noticed I was getting a little "belly." One evening I talked to Ray about the possibility of me being pregnant. He said maybe I should go to a doctor and find out for sure. So, Ray got an afternoon off and took me to a doctor at the U.S. Navy's Balboa Hospital. I was directed through at least three buildings before I actually saw a doctor! When the doctor finally appeared, he never asked me one question. He just said, "Is that a tracheotomy on your neck?" I said yes. Then he turned around, and as he was walking away, he said, "We don't want anything to do with somebody that is probably going to have problems in their pregnancy." He then turned to me and said, "Go find yourself any specialist you want, and the Navy will pay for it." I never did discover the answer to the question I had come to find out—if I was pregnant. I went back to the car and began to cry, but Ray told me not to worry, we would find a real good doctor to go to.

All kinds of thoughts were now going through my mind. I was wondering what the Navy doctor meant by "...was probably going to have problems." I didn't know any doctors in San Diego, so I asked Kay if she could recommend one. I talked it over with Ray, and we decided to go with her suggestion. One advantage to using this doctor was that his office was not very far from where we lived. I called the doctor and made an appointment. I was anxious to find out if I was pregnant. In a way, I was excited because I thought I couldn't have any children. In another way, I was worried that if I was pregnant, I would probably have to quit work, and we needed the money I earned to pay for food, and the nice apartment we had. In the meantime, I went to work every day, and worked as hard as I could to make my quota.

The day finally came when it was time to go to the doctor's office. Ray and I made test runs in our car to the doctor's office many times before the actual day of my appointment, to make sure I wouldn't get lost going to my appointment. I was scared driving by myself to the doctor's office, because I had to drive through a bad area of the city. The year before there were riots in this area and I imagined that the black people resented white people driving through their neighborhoods. I drove to the doctors without any problems, however, and even managed to be on time for my appointment. The doctor seemed real nice and spent a lot of time with me, and then told me he thought I would probably be having a baby around October 20.

    I could hardly wait to tell Ray what the doctor had to say. I was glad to have somebody say yes, you are pregnant. When I told Ray our good news he was very happy. He loved kids and said he always wanted to be a father someday. We both were concerned about not having enough money, but Ray assured me everything would be okay. The next day I told Kay I was pregnant. She was really happy for me—Kay and her husband wanted children and she just hadn't become pregnant yet. As weeks went by, work was getting harder and harder for me, especially because I could never sit down. I started gaining a lot of weight, and felt sick most of the time. At lunchtime, it was all I could do to get up on top of my table to eat my lunch. One day, Ray couldn't come home because he had to stand duty at the naval base. So, I drove home and sat on the couch and fell asleep. When I woke up, it was dark and the outside lights of the apartment building were on. I could see the shadow of a man wearing a big hat walking by my window, then he began turning my doorknob! I was so scared I froze for a minute, then I heard the side gate outside our apartment, and I remembered I hadn't closed the inside back door or locked it. I got up and started running toward the door, and just as I got there and locked the door, so did the man! Thank the Lord I was just a few seconds faster at getting to the door than he was! I was so scared, but didn't have a telephone, so I thought the best thing for me to do was to sit tight and hope he would go away. The man left, but I was so terrified that I sat up all night. As I was sitting in the dark, I realized I not only had myself to protect, but I had to think of the precious little baby that I was carrying. When morning came, I got up and took a shower, and got ready for work.

When I got to work the following day, I was exhausted from not having had any sleep the previous night. But, not sleeping at night occurred frequently now because of my pregnancy. I would have heartburn so bad, I would end up sleeping in a chair part of the night. I didn't tell anyone about the guy trying to get in my apartment that night. I figured everyone would just laugh and tell me I probably imagined everything. I had wished I imagined everything, because now I knew that even in this apartment building, I had to be sure my doors were locked at night.

One day at the factory, everyone was busy when all of a sudden you could hear women screaming at each other. I looked up from my work and watched one woman grabbing another woman by the hair, and throwing her to the floor. These two women went at each other for several minutes before the floor manager got to them and made them stop fighting. I had never seen two women fight before! These women were out to actually hurt each other. It took a while for everyone to get back to work. This meant less time for me to make my quota. I wasn't feeling very well and was starting to get depressed because I knew there wasn't any way I could make my quota that day. The girl across the table noticed I was struggling, and she said, "Here, take some of my tickets so you can meet your quota." I sure did appreciate her help! I knew what a good friend I had made, and I hoped there would be something that I could do for her someday.

As the weeks went by I grew bigger and bigger. The doctor told me I had a severe case of toxemia, and that I would have to stay off my feet and avoid salt. I didn't know what toxemia was, but I knew there was no way I could stay off my feet. Some days I could hardly make it through the day, and by the time I would get home, I would be so sick Ray would have to take me to the doctor. I would go into one of their little examining rooms, and lie down on a table and pass out. When I woke up the doctor would tell me I could go home. He never gave me anything, or offered suggestions as to what I could do. He would just say "Goodbye!" I thought his actions were kind of strange, but I figured that maybe this is just how it is when you're pregnant. I knew one thing for certain; I wouldn't be able to stand all day much longer!

The people in the factory office started teasing me about keeping a baby basket ready for me. One particular day it was very hot, and the steam press machines right behind me were rolling a lot of hot steam right on me. The girls at my table insisted that I work on the other side of the table, and one of the girls got a bench for me to sit on. It wasn't long before the floor manager noticed me sitting on the bench, and suggested I get off the bench right away. But the girls at my table put up such fuss for me! She said, "Oh, all right, just this one time."

Because I had gained so much weight, there were only a few maternity clothes that fit me well enough to wear to work. Often I would wear what I is known as "knee knockers," and I was reminded that I had to wear regular slacks. I tried to explain that I didn't have any slacks that fit me, and I hated to buy any more maternity clothes, because I didn't have much longer to work. She gave in and let me wear the clothes that I had. One particular night, when I was leaving work, a piece of material must have stuck to the bottom of my shoe. When I got to the stairs I began to fall, and instead of somebody trying to keep me from falling, everyone just cleared the way and let me fall down three flights of stairs. When I finally got to the bottom of the stairs, a woman asked if I was okay. I felt so ridiculous, I managed to get up and pretend everything was okay. In reality, I was in a lot of pain. I don't know how I made it to my car, but I managed to go and pick Ray up at the "nickel snatcher," the passenger ferry at the foot of Market Street. When he got in the car, he knew something was wrong. When I told him what had happened, he insisted that it was time to turn in my two weeks' notice, and this would give me some time to rest before the baby was due.

The next day, I took Ray to the ferry as usual, and then went to work. I didn't know if I could stand working another two weeks, but I sure had to try. When I fell down the stairs, it must have caused the baby to drop, and now it felt like the baby was lying right on my pelvis—this caused me a lot of pain. I wasn't sure why, but I thought it might have something to do with breaking my pelvis when I was in the car accident. With this added pain, along with everything else, I wasn't sure I would be able to stand up all day without passing out. When I got to work, I went straight to the office and gave my two weeks' notice. They seemed almost happy that I was going to quit! When I got to my table, the girls heard about me falling down the stairs the day before, and were all concerned about me. Then I told them that I was putting in my last two weeks. They all said they would do anything to help me get through the next days ahead. It was getting harder and harder for me. The girls were carrying my coats to me, and I never could make my quota. Everyone at my table gave me some of their slips every night. I was so grateful that I couldn't thank them enough.

One day while working, I almost passed out, and one of the girls went and got a stool for me to sit on for the rest of my shift. My supervisor came and told me to get off the stool, and the girls asked her to leave me alone. She just wheeled around, and to my surprise, she left. I made it through the rest of the morning. I was happy that my working days were almost over, but I felt kind of sad, because I was going to miss all the girls I worked with at my table. They were the only people I knew in San Diego, except for Kay. When lunchtime came on my last day at Ratner's, I couldn't get up on my table any more, so I looked for a little corner to sit down for a while. Suddenly people started coming from everywhere, putting gifts on the table, and then someone brought in a big cake. I couldn't believe it was for me. I didn't even know most of the women! Everyone was just great. I didn't have time to open my gifts because we only had a short lunchtime. This was just what the doctor ordered—it gave me enough energy to get through the rest of the day!

After work, Kay had made arrangements to get all of the gifts to my car. I could hardly wait to get home and look at all the presents I had received. Looking at the little baby things made the baby seem more real to me. It also scared me, because I started to realize how small a baby was! Ray had to stay on base that night, so I had plenty of time to go over and over all my presents. I hadn't bought anything for the baby yet. I figured I still had a month, and when I wasn't working, maybe I wouldn't be so tired all the time. I could hardly wait to show Ray all of our baby's new things! The next day, I slept in and to tell the truth, I think I slept most of the day. Ray was still on duty the next night, and all I had to worry about was myself.

The next morning, Ray was home. I didn't feel very well, and I had a hard time standing up, so Ray thought I had better call the doctor. The doctor thought I should come in right away, so I did. I made it as far as the stretcher in the doctor's office, and fainted. When I woke up, the doctor just said, "You can go now, you will be all right—stay away from salt, and don't eat any sugar." Now I had too much sugar in my system! But the doctor assured me this would probably go back to normal after I had the baby. So we went home feeling like the whole trip was a waste of time, because the doctor didn't seem to care one way or the other.

I had to go back to the doctor's office in a week. On my way to the doctor's, I was driving through the "rough" area, and a group of black men blocked my car at a stop sign, and began to rock it back and forth. I was so scared, and there wasn't anything I could do except pray they would quit and let me go! I just sat in my car with the doors locked—finally they quit rocking, started laughing, and walked away from my car. I took off as fast as I could, and thanked God they had left me alone. I'm not sure how I drove the rest of the way to the doctor's office, but somehow I managed!

It seemed like I was gaining too much weight, but the doctor didn't say anything about it. I had gained 60 pounds, and I still had almost a month to go before the baby was supposed to be born. I was bored most of the time, because I didn't know anyone, and Ray was on duty at the Naval Air Station, North Island, most of the time. We never had any money, now that I wasn't working, and one day when Ray was at work, there wasn't much to eat in the house. When he called me from work, I started to cry about not having enough food. He told me to take some money out of his coin collection, and walk to the store and buy what I wanted to eat. As soon as I hung up the phone I was out of the door, and on my way to the grocery store. I bought milk, bread and a package of cookies. When I returned home, I began my feast, and ate almost everything I had bought!

If Ray didn't put my shoes on before he went to work, I couldn't bend down far enough to put them on myself. One day, he didn't have time to put my shoes on before he left, and a girl from the factory had asked me to go to lunch with her. I couldn't find my shoes anywhere. I had almost given up on finding them, when I happened to open the refrigerator to get a pop. There were my shoes sitting in the refrigerator! Now I knew I was losing my mind! This was good for a laugh for quite a few days.

Ray finally had a day off, and there was a Canadian Navy destroyer tied up at the foot of Broadway. Ray wanted to go on a tour of the ship. I didn't think I felt well enough to go, but Ray convinced me I might feel better if I did some walking. Well, if I had any idea what I was in for, I never would have gone on a tour of that ship! It seemed like all I did was climb up and down a bunch of very steep stairs. By the time I got off the ship, I was really sick, and was sure I was going to have the baby right there—but of course, I didn't. We went home, and the first thing I did was eat, and then I just had to lie down.

That night, I woke Ray up, as I was feeling pretty bad, and was bleeding a little bit. He called the doctor, and the doctor said I had better go to the hospital. This was September 29, and the baby wasn't due until the middle of October. But I thought that I had better go to the hospital, just to be safe. By the time I got to the hospital, I was having labor pains. After I got signed in, we went to a room. I got undressed and got into a bed, but I wasn't sure what to expect next. I thought I was going to see a doctor. But instead, I started having labor pains about every three minutes. I thought I would probably have a few of these pains, have my baby, and everything would be back to normal. I was totally unaware of what was to follow!

After eight hours of hard labor pains, the doctor finally came in and gave me a "hypo." I didn't know what it was for, but later, after I had my baby, I found out that what he had given me was a shot that numbed me from the waist down to my feet. In recovery, I was really out of it for about four hours. I tried to talk and couldn't, and when they gave me my baby to hold, I couldn't hang on to her. I figured this was normal, because I wasn't sure what was supposed to be happening. I didn't have any concept of time, but I knew that Ray had left. A nurse came in and said in a mean voice, "Time to get out of bed." I thought she had to be kidding! My eyes wouldn't even focus yet! But, I decided I had better do what she told me to do.

So, I got out of bed and as I was rounding the end, I started to pass out. Then the nurse yelled, "What are you trying to do? You are going to break your stitches open!" I was surprised I had stitches; no one told me I was going to get stitches! Then I began to wonder just what the nurse wanted me to do. Then she said in a harsh voice, "Go into the bathroom, and read what you are supposed to do on the sheet of paper on the wall." I should have told her my eyes wouldn't focus, but by this time I was scared of her, and I didn't want to make her mad. So I went into the bathroom, and, of course, I couldn't read a thing, but I did see the paper with a message on the wall. So I stayed in the bathroom for a few minutes and came out. She was gone, so I got back into bed.

The next morning I got up and made it to the bathroom, and back in bed, before they brought my breakfast. I hadn't seen a doctor yet, since the birth of my little girl. But, I never thought anything of it, because, again, I thought that this is the way it is supposed to be! They finally brought my baby in, and I fed her for the first time. She was so small—I had never seen a new baby before, but I remembered to hold her head, and support her back. Then the nurse came and got her. I wondered what was I supposed to do next, but nobody came back, so I just went to sleep.

When I awoke, it was suppertime, and I began to wonder if I was going to get to see my little girl any more today. Ray came, and he had never seen her, so we thought we would walk down to the nursery and take a peek at our new little girl. I hadn't been out of bed all day long, and I almost fainted again, but I was determined to walk to the nursery.

When we looked at all the babies, we realized that our baby had red hair. We looked at her for a while, and then went back to the room. The next morning, the nurse came in with my baby, and told me I was taking her home at noon. Boy, was I scared now! I didn't know the first thing about what I was supposed to do. I called Ray and woke him up, as he had a party the night before at our apartment, and was sleeping in. I told him to come and get me, that I was coming home. I had never seen a doctor since I had my baby, and this seemed a little strange to me, but what did I know?

Ray finally came, and we got our baby dressed, and I was wheeled to our car carrying my new baby. I felt kind of funny because we couldn't get in the passenger side of the car, because it was still bolted shut from when we were in the car accident. So, the baby and I rode in the back seat of the car, with Ray driving in the front seat. This was not at all happening the way I had seen it in the movies!

I was unhappy that Ray was so late in picking us up, and then having to sit in the back by myself with the baby made me feel even worse. When we got home we brought our new little girl into her very first home, and we weren't quite sure what to do next. We named our precious baby Kathy, because she looked like a Kathy to us. It's kind of funny because we spent a lot of time going over names, and we decided if the baby was a girl we would call her Heather. Then, when she was born and we saw her, we knew she had to be named Katherine, Kathy for short.

Standing in our apartment with just Ray and the baby made me realize just how important family is. I didn't have anyone to share my excitement with, and to be able to say, "Look, everyone, isn't she just perfect." I wanted my family back home to see her so badly. But I knew it wouldn't help if I got depressed, so I tried to be cheerful. I was very tired and felt weak. Ray said to me, "Go and lie down and I'll wake you up when the baby wakes up." Then we all fell asleep—Ray, Kathy and me. The next time I heard anything was about three hours later, and Ray, with Kathy in his arms, was trying to wake me up. Ray had already put dry diapers on her, but wasn't quite sure about feeding her just yet. Up to this point, I had only given her one bottle of water. So I wasn't too sure myself. I took one look at this beautiful baby, and I knew that her whole life depended on us. It is funny, but instinct just takes over and suddenly you find yourself fixing a bottle, and feeding the baby, and burping and cuddling her, as if you knew what you were doing. I must have done okay, because Kathy fell fast asleep and looked so content.

A TALENT LOST/A LIFE WITH A PURPOSE

I loved the way baby Kathy smelled, and felt, and the way she would look at me—as if she already knew that I was her mother. Ray just adored her, and couldn't keep his hands off of her. It was our very first night with a baby in the house, and everyone had told us that we might as well get used to losing a lot of sleep. We were told that a baby kept you up all night. So we made a decision to take turns being up with her. But the next thing I knew, it was six o'clock in the morning and we had slept all night! I jumped out of bed thinking something must be the matter with Kathy, because she never woke up all night. But when I looked at her in her basket, she was just beginning to stretch and move around a little bit. Now I knew for sure that she was a keeper! What a good baby!

Ray was on leave for a week to help me with Kathy, until I could get back some of my strength. I was so glad to have him helping me that, by the end of the week, I felt petty good. I also had Kathy on a schedule, and it seemed to be working out pretty well. I felt I was getting the routine of being a mother figured out. I wanted to do everything perfectly. When it came to washing diapers, I wasn't going to let my baby have any stains on her diapers. I would fill three tubs of water, one to put them in soap, one to put them in bleach, and another tub to rinse the bleach out of them. Then I would put them in a washing machine, to wash them. When all the procedures were done I would hang them in the sun. I thought everyone did their diapers this way, until another lady asked me why I was doing so much work washing the diapers. After I started doing the wash in a more normal fashion, washing clothes wasn't such a chore.

Ray went back to work, and I became a stay-at-home mom. Now that I was home all the time, I began to meet some of the other people that lived in the same apartment building. Not only did I meet about six other women, they were all Navy wives and we all had babies almost the same age. Right away, I knew that I was going to enjoy having other women with the same interests, to visit with. It wasn't long before we all started getting together sometime during every day. It was so much fun watching all the babies interacting with each other. There usually was one or more of the women's husbands who had duty the same four days as Ray, and we would get together for supper, and to spend the evening. Sometimes we would all get into a car with our babies, and go to a mall. I couldn't believe I finally was actually having a good time in San Diego. It was nice because none of us had much money to buy a variety food, so we would all put our food together and come up with some really nice meals. Some of my favorite outings were trips to the San Diego Zoo. I knew Kathy would probably never remember she was ever there. But, we enjoyed taking her there anyway. The days seemed to go much faster, now that I had friends and a baby to take care of.

I'll never forget the first time I went grocery shopping at the commissary. The store was a supermarket just for military families. Everything at the store was inexpensive, because they tried to keep the prices low, knowing the servicemen didn't make very much money. The only drawback about it was that they wouldn't allow children in the store. They provided a nursery with nurses and staff for the families to leave their children while they shopped. When we went to drop off Kathy so we could grocery shop, I cried and cried. I just couldn't bear leaving her with strangers. We hurried through our shopping, and when we went to get her, she was sound asleep.

It was getting close to my 21st birthday, and Ray wanted me to see some of the places in San Diego that I wasn't old enough to go in before. We had never left Kathy with anyone except the Navy daycare while we grocery shopped. Luckily one of my girlfriends offered to keep her while we went out for my birthday. We decided to take her up on her offer. It had been a long time since we had been anywhere. Before Kathy was born we went to a couple of teenage nightclubs that didn't serve alcohol. We saw

Glenn Campbell perform at a concert before he had become nationally famous.

The day was December 1st, my birthday. The weather was warm and sunny outside, a lot different than the weather back home in Michigan. We hated leaving Kathy, but we were excited to be going out together just the two of us. I was so thrilled. I had a very handsome husband, and the night was gorgeous. Ray took me to several nightclubs, and we danced and just had fun. We knew it was getting late, but there was one more thing I wanted to do before the evening was over, and that was to walk along the pier and look at the ocean with the moon glistening on the water. It was beautiful. My birthday was perfect. Now I could hardly wait to go get back to our baby.

Christmas was just 24 days away. Christmas trees were expensive in California, which was something we never had to think about in the Soo. People usually just went out to the woods and cut their own tree. But in California you couldn't do that because they didn't have wooded areas with evergreen trees suitable for Christmas trees. The trees that were available were trucked here from elsewhere. The people who sold them could charge whatever the market would bear. They knew if you wanted a tree you would pay the price. We decided food was more important than a Christmas tree, so, I decorated a pole lamp with some decorations a friend gave us. It looked pretty, if I do say so myself! It made our little apartment look a lot more like Christmas, anyway. We decided not to buy each other anything much, because Kathy was present enough for the both of us.

This was going to be our first Christmas as a family. Wherever we went, everything was decorated so pretty, but there wasn't any snow and it seemed weird to be wearing shorts at Christmas time. Both sides of our family sent some gifts to put under our lamp. I knew we couldn't afford a big dinner like we were used to on Christmas Day, but maybe we could have tacos or something like that. Christmas came and we enjoyed just being together as a family. We went for a ride in the car and went to the zoo, which was just fine with me, because it was one of my most favorite places to go. The next day it was back to the same schedule as before Christmas. Ray went back to the base, and I stayed home with Kathy. Three or four of us girls got together and showed each other what we got for Christmas. Then we just sat around and played with all the babies.

Ray came home one day and said, "How would you like to get a bird?" He said his buddy had a parakeet and a cage to give away because he was being discharged from the Navy. I said, "Sure, let's try it." Ray's friend brought the bird over, and did the bird ever look unique. It had a pure white star right in the middle of his forehead.

We didn't let the bird out of its cage for the first few days until it got used to its new surroundings. Every day I would spend a lot of time talking to the bird. It seemed to be paying attention to me. Kathy would smile and make noises at the bird. After a week or so, I began to let the bird just fly around and then go back to its cage. When the bird was out, I would talk to it, but I never tried to touch him. One day, while I was working in the kitchen, the bird came and lit right beside me. I reached out and stroked the bird's feathers. Surprisingly, the bird sat and let me pet him. From that day on, the bird was very friendly. Another thing that was weird was that I never found any bird droppings anywhere, except in his cage.

The bird loved Kathy—it would follow her around, and land on her leg. The bird had a little bell, and he would bring the bell over to where Kathy was sitting on the floor. He would stand in front of her, and ring his bell by shaking his head back and forth. This was really funny to watch, and Kathy loved the attention the bird was giving her. One night several of us girls in Capri Terrace (the name of our apartment complex) got together for a "sleepover" in my apartment. Someone had been stealing clothes off the clotheslines at the common laundry area, and it made us feel kind of spooky when our husbands weren't home. So, we decided to stay together at night when we were alone. I told the girls not to worry, if anyone came to the door, the bird would start to make a lot of noise. After we had settled down all our babies, we were all fast asleep. We had made a bed on the living room floor for one of the babies. We were not expecting her to wake up during the night, because she was a sound sleeper. But, all of a sudden we heard the bird making a lot of screeching noises. Everyone jumped up and went running for the living room. The baby had awakened, and had crawled over to the birdcage, and was shaking it quite hard! The bird was frightened, and was letting everyone know it! When we saw what was happening, we all had a good laugh, and tried to get everyone back to sleep. That was a night to remember!

The Move to Marshall, Michigan

Ray and I talked it over, and decided that financially, the best arrangement would be for him to spend his last two months of duty in the Navy by himself, so we could save money for when he got out. It wouldn't cost anything for Ray to stay on base, and I could stay with my sister and her family in Marshall. This was going to be very hard for Kathy and me to leave San Diego without him. But the day of departure arrived, and there were many tears as Kathy and I boarded the plane to fly to Detroit, where my sister was going to pick us up. The plan included the two of us staying with my mother for a month in Sault Sainte Marie.

Kathy was just 18 months old, and I'm sure she missed her daddy as much as I did. But my sister, Joyce, was more than generous, opening up her home to two more people when she already had two kids of her own. She made us feel welcome, and did everything she could do to see that we were comfortable. Kathy seemed to be handling this big change in her life very well. We stayed at Joyce's for a month, and then Kathy and I went to my mother's house and waited for Ray to get out of the Navy. I bought a stroller, and walked all over every day. I think Kathy started to enjoy this routine. I was trying to make the days go faster so we could once again be with my man, and Kathy's daddy.

Staying busy worked. It was nearing the day when Ray was to come home, so we headed back to Marshall where we had decided to live. I was so happy to see Ray get off the plane when we picked him up in Detroit. I went running straight into his arms, where I had learned to feel so safe, and just plain comfortable. Kathy also was very excited to see her daddy. I could hardly wait to get our own little place to set up a home again. Unfortunately, we were broke and couldn't afford much. But, we found an apartment in a building we called the chicken coop, due to it being shaped like one. Before even looking at it I said let's get it, because the rental rate was so reasonable. So we moved into the upstairs unit, where there was just a living room, bedroom, and a bathroom with only a shower. The kitchen consisted of a counter with a sink in it at the end of the living room—period. It sure wasn't a pretty sight to see. But, the three of us were together again. I was very happy. The next day Ray went job hunting, and he found a job in nearby Battle Creek working at a Kroger super market, as a full-time clerk in the produce department. At least it was a job, and now we had an income.

Right away I started to look for a larger place where Kathy could have her own bedroom, and some room to play. We settled on a small house that was advertised in the paper as the "pumpkin special." It was near Halloween, and the house was orange. The purchase price was just $6,000, and the monthly payments were only $60. It turned out to be not such a great bargain. Shortly after moving in, we found out the furnace didn't work, and the windows wouldn't open. The walls had holes in them, so I got colored Kleenex and made roses, and stuck them in every hole. This also was an exciting time, because I was pregnant again. I was very happy, but I never felt well. Ray was not only working full-time, but was going to Kellogg Community College at night. We didn't get to see him much during the week, and on the weekends I didn't want to bother him by telling him how terrible I felt. I just wanted to be a happy family like we were in California. I just kept getting sicker and sicker, until one night I started to hemorrhage. I finally lost our baby, and felt very sad. But everyone else acted like it wasn't a big deal, so I just got on with my life. We lived in this house for a winter and nearly froze. Some days Kathy had to wear her snowsuit while inside the house. Right about the time we started looking for a better house to live in, I discovered that I was pregnant again. This time, it would last through to normal birth.

The day before our son Scott was born, we signed the papers to purchase a three-bedroom brick house. The very next morning, I went into labor. When I told Ray I was ready, he asked if I could just sit down for a few minutes while he showered and shaved. I guess he remembered how long he had waited in the delivery room when Kathy was born. My thoughts were that this is just great—here I'm having a baby, and he wants to get beautiful! So, while he was getting ready, I sat and counted contractions. Things progressed very quickly this time, and, luckily, we made it to the hospital. We had a beautiful baby boy, and named him Scott. The day finally came when I could take him in my arms, and care for him as I did for Kathy. I was so happy to have this baby after losing one, and I had worried that I would never have any more children. I said a little prayer, and thanked the Lord for my bundle of joy.

When we got home, Kathy was waiting eagerly. We had never left her for more than a couple of hours before, and she was glad to see us. Since she had been the only child for four years, we brought her home a baby of her own. It was a doll that was popular at the time, called Mrs. Beasley. Kathy was happy to get the doll, but she wasn't sure of the other little bundle I was carrying. I immediately sat her on the couch, and let her hold Scott, hoping they would bond. Kathy wasn't sure she wanted to do that either, so I decided it might be better to give her a little time to get used to him being in our home.

When I entered this house, everything was new to me. I had only seen the inside of the house for a few minutes, when we were deciding if we wanted to buy it. Ray had moved all of our belongings and furniture into the house while I was in the hospital with Scott. Not only did I have a new baby, I was now in a house where I didn't know where anything was. I was just so happy to be with Kathy and my new baby that it didn't matter, as I felt I now had a perfect family. I had a husband that I adored, and a perfect little girl and boy—I couldn't imagine that anyone could ever want more. I felt like I was in heaven on earth with everything God had made possible for me.

By the time Scott was a year old, Ray had finished his associate's degree in business administration, and was working as an inside salesman for a small manufacturer. Due to mismanagement, the company was failing, and Ray soon lost his job. Within a couple of weeks, however, Ray had another job with State Farm Insurance Companies as a senior underwriter in the auto insurance division. We soon got involved with the local Jaycee chapter, where we could work on local projects, and learn leadership development. We were also busy with our children, and making many new friends from our contacts in the Jaycees. Things seemed to be prospering, and we found a great ranch home near where Ray worked, and two doors away from an elementary school. We were moving once more, into another home with a big fenced-in back yard.

Jaycees/Jaycee Auxiliary

As I mentioned, Ray had the opportunity to join the Jaycee chapter in Marshall, Michigan. We knew very little about the organization, but felt that it was a good way to get involved in the community. Ray was first encouraged to join by his coworkers. He had been in the Jaycees for several months when one of the wives called and asked me to join the JC Auxiliary. This was all new to me. Up until now I had stayed home with my children, and tried to be "Mrs. Suzy Homemaker"! The thought of getting out and just talking to other women seemed like a great idea to me. When I went to my first meeting I was really amazed at how much they did for the community. I could hardly wait to get started working on a Jaycee Auxiliary project.

Our group ran a bingo for charity once each week, and we had a haunted house for Halloween every year, in which Ray and I were both involved. We ran numerous projects. I chaired "Dessert with the Easter Bunny," in which I was the Easter Bunny, and I also went around to all the grade school classrooms dressed as the Easter Bunny. During the week before Easter, we held a program at the civic center where the kids could come and put frosting on sugar cookies, and talk to the Easter Bunny. There were games and prizes for all. We also held an Easter egg hunt for all of the town's children at the fairgrounds. To this day, Marshall still runs this project for the kids. At Christmas time, the guys disposed of every Christmas tree set out at the curb on the second Sunday in January. There were other projects like painting an entire house for someone who didn't have the means to hire it done.

A TALENT LOST/A LIFE WITH A PURPOSE

The Jaycees delivered baskets of food to the needy, sold apple cider door-to-door in the fall, and chaired a "toys for tots" program for Christmas. One special project that Ray co-chaired was the reconstruction of a public park in the downtown area. It included new sidewalks, park benches, and a pineapple-themed fountain in the center. President Gerald Ford's son came to dedicate its completion, then we went to Win Schuler's famous restaurant to have lunch with him.

The men's and ladies' Jaycee meetings were held separately. Being with a group of women was good for me. We had our own leadership, project chairwomen, and motivational meetings. This was the very first place I ever talked about my car accident to anyone. One evening, at the home of the chairperson for a women's leadership forum, we were all taking turns telling about something bad that had happened in our lives. I can remember starting to shake and couldn't speak very well. However, everyone was very patient while I got my story out. This was the beginning of being able to talk about the accident.

I was glad to get it off my chest. It had been seven years since the car wreck, and never once had I been able to discuss it freely. I made a nice group of friends through these sessions, and from working on the many projects we ran in the community. Before we left the group, Ray was honored as a lifetime member of Jaycees International, and designated as a JCI Senator for his contributions to the organization. This is quite an honor and I felt very proud of him.

Moving On

I'm going to try to explain the problems a serious car accident can do to a person's body.

First, as I see it, a bad car wreck not only does physical damage, it affects your mind, soul and your being. A person carries this extra baggage with them the rest of their life. The best way to explain it, I think, is to think of totaling your car. A mechanic can work on your car, but nothing quite lines up anymore. The engine sounds good, but there still are problems of doors not fitting just right, the lights not working right, and maybe it just doesn't go down the road as straight as it used to. So, you have those things fixed, but you find yourself constantly having to take it in for repairs. Sometimes you just feel like "junking" the car.

The problem with humans is that we can't just junk ourselves. So, it is a never-ending job of getting repairs. I want to quit thinking about the accident, but it is clear that I was never "junked out." I personally refuse to sit by idly. Challenges have sprung up in my life, and I choose to face each one, and overcome the obstacles to the best of my ability. I understand that issues will arise where you are walking a fine line of trying to keep everything as normal as possible, but never quite feeling just right about yourself or how your body is functioning. A strong will, determination, and faith in God will serve as mechanic's tools in enriching one's life.

There are times when you must trust your instincts, and learn to persevere in the face of rejection. For instance, I have been to many doctors over the years, and I found that doctors can be cruel. At one time, I was going to one eye specialist after another for answers about my eyesight. I wasn't able to read a book or newspaper. One particular eye doctor looked at me and said, "You look like a young person that has had a stroke." Before I could explain anything to him, he had me sit at his desk and turn my head to the side. He proceeded to poke my arm with straight pins to see if he could get a reaction. He was poking my left arm, which didn't have much feeling in it. So he yelled, "Can't you feel this?" I looked at him to see what he was talking about. That's when I discovered he had been poking my arm with straight needles. He got up and said there was nothing he could for me.

I didn't give up—I just knew there was somebody who could help me. The next eye doctor I went to told me I had a tumor behind my eye. I was very upset. So I took the next step and had an x-ray of my eye. Everything was normal. I kept going to eye specialists, and I finally found a doctor in Marshall, Michigan, who spent three hours examining my eyes! He found my eyes were partially paralyzed, and had palsy (a condition, caused by my car accident, where the eye was constantly moving). He searched, and found an eyeglass prescription that would allow me to read. To this day, I continue to consult Dr. James Fletcher. He is truly a very caring person, and an excellent eye doctor.

I also experience some ongoing problems with my jaws, as a result of them having been broken in four places. An oral specialist told me he would like to do surgery, but it would leave a nasty scar on my face. I chose not to have the surgery, whereupon he screamed at me, "Some day you will be back in so much pain, but don't expect me to help you then." I still have not had any surgery on my jaws, and this incident happened many years ago.

Also, problems with my ears have caused me to go to many different specialists for help. Both of my eardrums were broken in the car accident, and I was left with holes in my eardrums that constantly made a whistle. I found this very hard to live with. Finally the holes closed by forming scar tissue. It was wonderful to talk to a person and not be distracted by the whistling noise. However, a few years later I was experiencing ringing in my ears, so I went to a local doctor. When he went to examine my ears, he saw an extra piece of skin in my ears and, without telling me what he was going to do, he put small scissors in my ear and cut the piece of skin he saw, re-opening the hole. Now I once again have a hole in my eardrum.

On Leading a "Normal Life"

Despite the enormous physical and emotional challenges I faced, I knew that I wasn't just fighting for myself. I was fighting to show the world that miracles could happen. If I could set an example, and give just one person hope, then my suffering will have served a purpose. I was determined to let the world know that the human spirit can overcome insurmountable obstacles. The first thing a person has to do is to never allow that word "impossible" in their vocabulary. When overcoming a setback, think of everything as an opportunity to show exactly what you're made of. I would be lying if I didn't admit it is hard work just to try to be normal after an accident like I had. But what you get for all your hard work is feeling really, really good about yourself, knowing that you beat all the odds the doctors had given you.

I walked across the stage without crutches to receive my high school diploma, just three months after the accident. I married my high school sweetheart just short of two years after the accident. I gave birth to two beautiful children, and raised them to adulthood. I struggle with claustrophobia, and I fear shots in the dentist's chair because the numbness might shut off my breathing—so I have had fillings and even root canal work without a painkiller. As I sit here today, writing my story, I still have every one of those broken bones from that fateful night in March of 1963—broken toe, broken pelvis, fractured collar bone, shattered jaw, cracked skull, and more. I still have problems, but I fix them and I get on with my life. One important lesson I have learned is that one must realize that the former "you" is never coming back. But now you have a chance to make the "new you" even better. God gave you another chance—live like He would choose you to. Be kind, courteous, thoughtful, patient, and loving to all men and women alike. If a limb doesn't have feeling, keep moving it, and using your hands and fingers just like you do with your full-functioning limb. Never leave your affected hand lying in your lap; put it on the table like your good hand, and through hard work, soon it may start functioning like it should. My greatest wish is to see everyone fight for his or her life, and for quality in that life. I can attest that the rewards are great, and I hope that someday, for those who are functionally challenged, someone will come up to you and say, "You are really a miracle!"

Meaning in Your Life

I have taken you on a journey through part of my life. I am now 60 years old, so there are a number of life experiences I didn't include in this memoir. But, on this the final page, I want to share with you what I consider to be two of the most wonderful miracles of my life—my beautiful daughter, Katherine, and my handsome son, Scott. I am so proud of both of them. Kathy has always shown a natural business management sense, and is currently the office manager for a large national heating/ventilation contractor in Battle Creek, Michigan. Scott is a local radio personality in the twin Sault area, and enjoys any chance to "ham it up," or get behind a microphone in front of a crowd (even at his own wedding!). Ray and I live in Sault, Michigan, enjoy our cabin on a lake in Strongs, Michigan, and are looking forward to retirement. We look forward to spending more time with each other, with our children, and with our grandchildren.

If my story, my spoken words, or a touch of my hand can comfort or give hope to others, I will know that God's purpose for me has been fulfilled.